GROWING UP
COUNTRY

ALSO BY CHARLIE DANIELS

Ain't No Rag: Freedom, Family, and the Flag

GROWING UP COUNTRY

What Makes Country Life Country

{ Edited by Charlie Daniels }

FLYING DOLPHIN PRESS

BROADWAY BOOKS

NEW YORK

PUBLISHED BY BROADWAY BOOKS / FLYING DOLPHIN PRESS

Copyright © 2007 by Charlie Daniels

All Rights Reserved

Published in the United States by Broadway Books, an imprint of The Doubleday Broadway Publishing Group, a division of Random House, Inc., New York. www.broadwaybooks.com

BROADWAY BOOKS / FLYING DOLPHIN PRESS and its colophon, are trademarks of Random House, Inc.

Book design by Caroline Cunningham

Essay by Senator Alexander: From *Six Months Off* by Lamar Alexander. Copyright © 1988 by Lamar Alexander. By permission of William Morrow, an imprint of HarperCollins Publishers. Essay by Deborah Allen: Lyrics reprinted courtesy of Curb Music/Posey Publishing Company. Essay by Dobie Gray: Material reprinted from *Dobie Gray* (Jay Warner Associates, 2007).

Library of Congress Cataloging-in-Publication Data
Growing up country: what makes country life country / edited by Charlie Daniels.—1st ed.
p. cm.
1. Country musicians—United States—Biography. 2. Country music—History and criticism. I. Daniels, Charlie, 1936– II. Title.

ML394.G85 2006
781.642092'273—dc22
[B]
2006034849

ISBN: 978-0-385-51846-8

PRINTED IN THE UNITED STATES OF AMERICA

1   3   5   7   9   10   8   6   4   2

First Edition

Dedicated to Hazel and Charlie

My wife and boy

My sun and moon

Contents

FAITH

HARD WORK

STARS AND STRIPES

THE GREAT OUTDOORS

MUSIC

HOME

Acknowledgments

So many of the people who have contributed to this book live hectic, busy lives and are constantly called on to do something like this. I just want to personally thank each and every one of them for taking the time to help make this project special.

God Bless.

Introduction

In retrospect it seems a kinder, gentler place, the world that I was born into on October 28, 1936, in Wilmington, North Carolina—a time when hugging was in style and a man's word was as good as any contract a Philadelphia lawyer could draw up.

Streetcar tracks still ran down the main thoroughfares of my hometown, and families sat around big floor-model radios together listening to *Fibber McGee and Molly* and the *Grand Ole Opry*.

Wilmington was a town of around thirty-three thousand people in those days, and we lived a few miles to the east of it on the Carolina Beach Road in a little clapboard house with electricity but no running water. Our sanitary facility was a short walk from the back door, and yes, folks, it's true, the old Sears and Roebuck catalog did spend its dotage in the little house out behind the big house, growing thinner by the day and titillating the imagination of little boys who sat there ogling the scantily clad models in the lingerie section.

I guess we would have been considered poor by today's standards, but everybody else was in the same boat, so we just didn't know any better. My daddy was a timberman, and my mother was a full-time housewife and mother.

Among the first things I remember is my first snowfall. The

flakes were as big as goose feathers to my infant eyes, and my grandmother cut off a pair of my uncle's old pants and sewed the cuffs together so they fit across the bottoms of my shoes so I could play out in it, my first snowsuit. I loved the snow then, and I still do to this day.

My streets were the wooded paths and my playgrounds were the fields, and watching out for snakes was a natural reaction in my bare-foot life; I'm so thankful that I came up that way. I grew up country before mega-pollution, when the stars were diamond chips on a piece of black velvet and a full October moon would bathe the land-scape in pure buttery silvery light, the tall longleaf pine trees casting their long, proud shadows, and the damp summer air was perfumed with magnolia and honeysuckle. And in the winter we left our tracks in a heavy frost across a field of brown Bermuda grass.

But growing up country is more than just having the good luck to be born in a particular geographic location or coming of age in a rural setting or making your living behind a plow. It's an attitude that's been woven into the fabric of my life, affecting every thought and every action.

There's an old saying that goes "Don't get above your raising." It's good advice and country philosophy at its finest. Never forget your roots, your values, your family, old friends, and the people who raised and nurtured you. I never did.

Growing up country means walking down the aisle with a grad-uating class of twenty-one of your closest friends to the melancholy strains of "Pomp and Circumstance" and out into a world you know very little about, but a world where the lessons of honesty, self-reliance, and a solid work ethic would stand you in good stead no matter where the slippery paths of ambition would lead you.

One of my fondest memories is of sitting on the front porch in my granddaddy's lap, safe, secure, and loved.

My mother could wield a switch with the aplomb of an

Olympic fencer, and as long as my infraction was minor, she would dole out the corporal punishment. But if I stepped too far over that fragile line, she would bring out the big guns. "We'll just wait until your daddy gets home."

Oh no, not that! It was bad enough to get a switching, but to have to dread it all day made it much worse. My parents never gave me a lick I didn't deserve, and I thank God that I had a momma and daddy who loved me enough to teach me right from wrong. One of the first lessons I learned is that everybody has to work, and that meant there was always a menial job around even for a good-sized toddler. My very first responsibility was bringing in split pine wood for my momma's big black cookstove, and if the wood box was empty, I was in big trouble.

Farming, especially in those days, when almost everything was done by hand, was a labor-intensive business, and there were no unions, no pensions, and no medical plan. If something got done, you did it yourself.

You soon learned that the health of those green things growing out of the ground decided what kind of life you and your family were going to have. There can be no shirking because there's always more than enough to keep everybody busy and there's nobody else to do your part. You grow up fast on a farm. I got my first very own shotgun the Christmas I was twelve years old. Hunting was a rite of passage in my family, and I'll never forget sitting around a fire waiting for the coon dogs to tree and listening to men with sun-ripened faces talk about the hunts they'd been on and the characters they'd known.

I am a child of World War II, and my feelings of patriotism were formed and forged at a time when everybody was patriotic, when America was straining every nerve to defeat Hitler and Hirohito. Everybody did their part, even the kids would collect tin cans and junk metal.

To me, patriotism is not a blind allegiance to some political party or ideology. It's wanting what's best for the country. Nobody's right all the time and nobody's wrong all the time, and the greatness of America is not found in Washington, D.C., but in the workplaces, nurseries, factories, and farms.

Now, I don't want to give you the wrong impression. We knew how to enjoy ourselves, too. We took off at twelve o'clock on Saturday and went to town just like everybody else in the county did. Saturday was a wondrous day, a country boy's delight, when Momma went grocery shopping and the kids went to the picture show and small southern towns were full of the good folks, men in clean bib overalls sitting around the barbershop talking about a big black bear somebody had killed and ladies standing in knots on the street discussing a mutual friend's recent surgery.

Of course we didn't work on Sunday. Sunday was the Lord's day and we observed it. I would be woke up all sleepy-headed to get ready to go to Sunday school, and then come home to eat fried chicken and chocolate cake for Sunday dinner, which to us was the midday meal.

Sunday was also visiting day. My grandma's yard would be full of cars as neighbors and kin came together to socialize. Eventually one of the ladies would sit down at my grandma's old upright piano and the singing would begin. They sang the old songs and the hymns and lifted their voices in unabashed joy, relishing the company of friends and kinfolks, and then family by family they'd pay their respects and drift away to get ready for another week of hard work.

Music has always been a big part of my life, and it seemed that practically everybody in my world listened to the *Grand Ole Opry* on Saturday nights. The six-hour radio broadcast from Nashville, Tennessee, over the fifty-thousand-watt clear-channel voice of WSM radio, boomed into coastal Carolina as clear as a bell. Monday morning you'd hear folks buzzing about what they'd heard Saturday night. "Did you hear Roy Acuff sing 'Great Speckled Bird'? Minnie Pearl was so funny I thought I'd pass out."

In those days country music truly was the music of the common man, the workingman, the honest man. The songs reflected the everyday joys and problems of the blue-collar crowd. Uncle Dave Macon sang about "ten-cent cotton and forty-cent meat, how in the world can a poor man eat?" Ernest Tubb's "Soldier's Last Letter," Hank Williams's "Your Cheatin' Heart." Common emotions, common problems, common man's music.

Yes, the *Grand Ole Opry* made an impression on almost everybody, but nobody took it more seriously than me. It represented a fantasy world that at the time seemed unapproachable, as far away as Pluto. But a boy can dream, and one day, when I showed up at my friend Russell Palmer's house, that dream was put in motion.

Russell was messing with an old Stella guitar and actually knew about two and a half chords on it. Well, I just about went nuts. I don't know how long he'd had that guitar or where he ever learned those chords, but what I did know was that he just had to teach them to me.

That day and that old Stella guitar changed my life forever. After I learned enough to play whole songs, I was obsessed with being a professional musician, which in North Carolina at that time was tantamount to finding gold. There was no place to play, with the exception of a few square dances and fiddlers' conventions. But I was determined, and as my life unfolded, I would find a way to pursue my dream.

This book holds the experiences and aspirations of many people who had the courage to chase their dreams. The essays are humorous and touching, and tell about the lives of everyday people who decided to march to a different drummer.

I hope in reading it that you will first of all be entertained, but as you realize that they're just everyday people, I hope that you will also be encouraged and motivated to follow your heart to the place you want to go.

I've had many things happen to me since my young days in North Carolina, things that I didn't even have the imagination to dream about way back then. All the accolades, awards, honors, and successes I've had I attribute to the blessings of Almighty God, a loving family, a belief that it's not how many times you get knocked down but how many times you get up, and, last but not least, growing up country.

Charlie Daniels

STARTING
OUT

Jared Ashley

As soon as he laid his hands on a guitar emblazoned with Mickey Mouse across the front, Jared Ashley knew what he wanted to do for the rest of his life. Never mind that he was only five years old at the time, he was hooked on making music. But it wasn't until years later, while he was serving in the Navy, that his fate was sealed. Sitting on a ship in the middle of the ocean, Jared stared out into the still blue waters and began to write songs.

Encouraged by his fellow soldiers, who hollered for more during impromptu jam sessions, Jared went on two Persian Gulf Department of Defense tours, where he performed for thousands of military personnel around the world. Once he got out of the Navy, he headed straight to Nashville to live out his dream. With unshakable determination and without a penny to his name, Jared assembled his Dirty South Band and landed a permanent gig at the city's legendary Tootsies Orchid Lounge, where he shared the stage with Merle Haggard, ZZ Top, Blues Traveler, and Toby Keith. Millions of viewers were introduced to Jared's high-energy country rock when he was a contestant on the fourth season of USA Network's popular show *Nashville Star*.

It took going halfway across the world for me to find my country roots. After I graduated from high school, I had no idea what I wanted to do. I'd just come off doing the Texas–New

Mexico tour circuit. I hadn't made a dime and I was tired. *Screw it*, I thought, *there's gotta be something better than this*. I knew there was life outside of my hometown, so I joined the Navy and figured I was giving up on music. I ended up spending four years overseas. I wanted to see the world and I did. And you know what I learned? People in America should be so proud to be born American. There's nothing that you can't do here.

After boot camp, I was stationed in Japan, and I'd sit on our ship playing acoustic guitar to pass the time. You have a lot of time on your hands when you're out at sea. Soon, all the country boys on the ship made their way over whenever I was playing. North Carolina, Nebraska, Georgia, Alabama—they were *real* country boys. We came from different places, but we were the same, too. We all came from good families, and we'd all worked our asses off. We formed a tight group pretty quick. Then we found George's Country Bar, right outside the base in Yokosuka, Japan. We all started hanging out there, and I asked George if I could play on Sunday nights. With my harmonica and guitar out there in Yokosuka, I rediscovered my love for playing music. One of my Navy buddies had a connection in Nashville. His grandfather was in the music business, so one day I sang for him over the phone. He asked me to make a demo tape. I sat in the bathroom on the ship with a tape recorder, while everybody in my division stood outside being real quiet. You could hear a pin drop—until an aircraft took off from the flight deck. But the tape was good enough, and my friend's grandfather told me to come to Nashville as soon as I could.

When I got out of the Navy, I moved to New Mexico, where my family was living. It was tough. My best friend from high school was still working at Subway five years later. My parents were still having the same arguments. Everybody from high school was hanging out at the same bars talking about the same things. The girls got pregnant and had to stay in town. The guys all worked for their fathers. It was like a spiderweb, being back home, and I didn't want to get stuck in it. I stayed in my bedroom for the first three weeks I was home, and on one Friday night I decided I'd had enough. I packed one bag, grabbed my guitar, jumped in my truck, and drove to Nashville.

Thanks to a friend from the Navy, I got a job in a bank doing security and investigations. But I still didn't have enough money for a place to live. I called up my dad, bought his Suburban, and slept in it until I was able to get a house. In the middle of winter. I slept in that damn thing until the heater coil went. Before I left New Mexico, I was smart enough to apply for a Texaco card. If it weren't for that card, I would have gone hungry or froze. Every day I headed to that gas station to buy hot dogs and fill my truck's tank so I could leave it running all night long to stay warm. I was in pretty bad shape. My boss insisted that we all be clean-shaven, so I spent a lot of my day just avoiding him. Finally, one day he pulled me aside and said, "Jared, when you got this job you knew our policy and you looked great. You had your military haircut and your suit and tie. But now you've got a beard and you just look awful. What the hell's wrong with you?" I told him my situation, that I didn't have a place to live, that I didn't even have enough money for razors. I was just trying to survive until my first couple of paychecks. He gave me twenty dollars, and I worked there for three and a half years.

I started playing six nights a week, from six to ten o'clock and from ten o'clock to two in the morning. I played as much as I could. I got off work at seven, and my band had started at six, so I'd try to bail out of work early, pull up to the bar downtown on Broadway, change out of my suit and into my Wranglers, and

jump up on that stage. I moved to Nashville to play country music because I loved country music. I didn't move to Nashville to be
a big star. I moved there to play music for a living. After traveling
around the world, searching for what I wanted in life, I had finally
found it.

Ray Benson

At six feet seven inches, Ray Benson cuts a striking presence onstage, and he's got the musical chops to back it up. As front man (and sole remaining founding member) for the nine-time Grammy-winning Western swing collective Asleep at the Wheel, the prolific master of Texas music has been performing and touring for over thirty-five years while also finding the time to make more than twenty albums. In the band's early years, the members lived together on a fully functional West Virginia farm, working on the land and gaining an understanding of the nuances of country life that influenced their music. At Willie Nelson's invitation, the band relocated to Austin, Texas, where it remains based today. In 2003, Ray released his solo album, *Beyond Time*, which earned two Grammy nominations. The toe-tapping, ever-jamming crew is currently traveling the country performing *Ride with Bob*, a musical play written and performed by the band members about the legendary King of Western Swing Bob Wills and the Texas Playboys.

I was a kid in the suburbs, but I didn't know it. We lived right on the edge of open country, so as far as I was concerned, I thought I was a country kid. I was in the 4-H club, I had a Jersey—she was the best milk cow around—and for most of my youth I ran around thinking I was a cowboy. Or Davy Crockett, roaming the country and bringing home every animal that I could trap or catch. My mom thought it was very cool until a ringneck snake got loose in the house. But he was just a little guy, and he wasn't even poisonous.

It didn't hit me what *real* country was until I was eighteen years old and, with a tax refund of fifty bucks, moved with some friends to Paw Paw, West Virginia. We worked out a great deal where we could stay on a fifteen-hundred-acre apple and peach orchard in exchange for caretaking. There were two houses and a two-hundred-year-old log cabin on the property. We hauled freshwater from the spring instead of turning on a tap and used kerosene lamps instead of electricity. We kept warm thanks to a woodstove. We were basically living like it was the eighteenth century. We rode horses all over—mine was named Hillbilly—and we kept busy clearing brush and repairing buildings. My friends and I had the run of the place, and we kept convincing more friends to join us. That's how Asleep at the Wheel was started. We'd been living on the farm for a couple weeks and playing music any chance we could when Lucky, the steel guitar player, came running out of the outhouse shouting, "I've got it! I know what our name is—Asleep at the Wheel!" I have no idea how he came up with it or what it means, but it's stuck all this time. When we weren't out hunting for our dinner, canning vegetables from the garden, or working on the land, we were cranking up the generator for band practice.

We had this idea that we wanted to really live. To see what it was like to fend for ourselves in the country. We sure found out. After two years, and countless missed gigs thanks to our van getting stuck in the mud bogs (the van was the one modern convenience we kept), we realized that old-fashioned life was hard. Real hard. So, with a new appreciation of the hardships of honest country living, we got back on the road, glad to have the lessons we learned to guide us.

Ross Coleman

You could say Ross Coleman was a natural-born cowboy. There's no doubt that a daredevil streak runs in his blood. His father and hero, Steve, was an accomplished bull rider, and his sister, Bridgett, is in the Cowgirl Hall of Fame. At just seven years old, Ross climbed onto his first calf. That same year the pint-sized champion in the making won his first buckle. With a sprawling cattle ranch in Oregon as his training ground, Ross rode every second he could. An adrenaline junkie who takes bull riding to the extreme, he pushed himself to his limits and quickly rose in the hardscrabble world of rodeo. In 2001, his name became synonymous with the richest eight seconds in bull-riding history during his awe-inspiring ride on Copenhagen Tuff-E-Nuff, the meanest bull he had ever seen. When he's not driving cattle with his dad or taming a bull on the circuit, this extreme cowboy can be found getting his rush riding a snowboard or jumping out of a plane.

It was springtime on the ranch, which meant it was time for the branding run. All the cattle got their shots, and the calves were branded. I was seven years old, and I was ready to ride my first calf. I got a lead rope around its belly, and the grown-ups helped me get on and turned me loose in the middle of the ring. I didn't last more than three or four jumps before getting drilled pretty hard, but I thought it was the most fun I'd ever had. I was hooked.

I worked my way up from little Shetland ponies to bucking horses, from calves to Black Angus cross bulls. Riding my favorite horse, Shotgun, around the ranch, I kept busy with the chores my dad gave me.

Once I got to high school, I started riding Peanut Butter. At twenty years old, he's still around today and is the most famous horse in town. We bought him for roping, but he kept bucking everyone off. We got fed up with him, so we just put him in the bucking chute for practice as a saddle bronc. For a couple years he was great to practice on, but one day he got tired of it and decided he wanted to go back to being a roping horse. He's still got a little buck left in him, and every now and then when you're roping, he'll let you know it.

I don't remember a day when I wasn't on horseback, working the cows or heading off to a rodeo. Our ranch has all the stock you can imagine, plus outdoor and indoor arenas with bucking and roping chutes. Thanks to my dad, I was given every opportunity to train, compete, and pursue my dream of being a professional bull rider. Once I built my confidence up on the Black Angus cross bulls, my dad bought more bulls that bucked harder. After school my friends would come over and we'd ride all afternoon. Every Wednesday during high school we'd each throw ten bucks in a pool for whoever would ride the best that day. We were riding ten steers a day—six- and seven-hundred-pounders, which were real docile compared with what I get on now.

In 2001, I rode one of the baddest bulls in the country— Copenhagen Tuff-E-Nuff was known as a big-time eliminator. Every time I ride a bull my adrenaline goes crazy, but it was pumping twice as much that day. My hero, Ty Murray, helped me get on him, and right before he pulled my rope down, he looked me in the eye and said, "Go psycho, Ross. Get out there, be a cowboy, and just go psycho." So that's what I did. I matched that bull move for move, and I knew there was no way he was going to throw me off. I covered that bull, and twenty thousand people in the stadium went nuts. It was the best feeling of my life. All the years of training on the ranch finally paid off. And it never would have happened without my family's support.

Joe Ely

Born on Route 66 to a family full of railroad workers, Joe Ely was destined to be a highway man. But the dry plains of west Texas have always run deep in his heart, and the mental snapshots of his upbringing blaze as brightly today as they did fifty years ago. Watching Jerry Lee Lewis perform on a flatbed trailer during an Amarillo dust storm, six-year-old Joe was amazed when the microphone blew over and the restless crowd had to resort to covering their faces with bandannas. A rebel at heart, he rode a motorcycle down the hallways of Monterey High School on the first day of his freshman year and was expelled for singing "Cherry Pie" at a school assembly. His spontaneous antics weren't fit for a classroom. They were fit for a stage. From his 1972 debut with the Flatlanders to his remarkable solo career, Grammy-winning Joe's life as a genre-mixing troubadour has taken him around the world and back again. Back to Texas, where he lives today. Thirty years after their debut album, the Flatlanders returned to the studio and emerged with the critically acclaimed *Now Again*. The trio's triumphant return was followed up with 2004's *Wheels of Fortune*.

My daddy died when I was twelve, and my whole life changed. Until then, there was a big emphasis on family, but after he died, my mother was sent off to a mental institution; she just couldn't quite handle it. I became the breadwinner of the family, washing dishes and cooking after school to make ends meet. I started playing in a band because it was a hell of a lot better than washing dishes. By the time I was fifteen, we were playing old honky-tonks and beer joints. Though in Lubbock, which was a dry town, they were actually bootleg joints—old places where you'd have to drive sixty miles to the nearest liquor store for a half-pint of gin. You could always count on finding someone out in the parking lot with a trunkful of booze for sale.

I was into all kinds of music when I met my Flatlander buddies Jimmie Dale Gilmore and Butch Hancock. Jimmie turned me on to the whole world of country music, and Butch turned me on to this whole folk world. I was in the rock-and-roll world, and I started seeing things from a different perspective. In the 1960s, everything just got real. I had thought west Texas was a place I could let my imagination run free, but it wasn't until I left that I realized there was a whole other world out there. And I didn't have to go too far to find it. In fact, I didn't even have to leave Texas. We headed to Austin, and it was completely different from everything I had known. You'd see Flaco Jiménez and Stevie Ray Vaughan jamming one night, B. B. King and Charlie Sexton the next night. Austin was a mecca of all different kinds of thoughts and ideas, all different kinds of music coming together. It made changes happen, and new forms of music arose from it.

After the Flatlanders, I recorded two albums I thought were country—interesting lyrics about life, steel guitar—but they flopped. I was sent on a tour of fairs, but the band just did not fit in. Suddenly we got word that the album was going up the charts in England. We headed over there and did full tours with Merle Haggard, Carl Perkins, and Bo Diddley. It was unbelievable. After two years, I hooked up with the Clash. They loved old rockabilly stuff—Marty Robbins songs about El Paso and Laredo and gunfighter ballads. I brought them to Texas during their first U.S.

tour, selling out in every city. Still, the audience looked at them like they were from Mars. We headed back to Europe. The scene there was perfect for me—it seemed like walking into this melting pot of music that was heavily influenced by Buddy Holly. So there I was, from Buddy's hometown of Lubbock, finding the true sound of my music and my Texas roots all the way across the Atlantic.

But I couldn't shake Texas out of my blood. I'm a fifth-generation Texan, and I've made Austin my home for years. I don't head back to west Texas very much, but it's the place I return to whenever I start a new album. I go back there, and I get on those old roads where you can drive for fifty miles without seeing a house. That feeling of wide-open space where you can see the horizon line 360 degrees around you—you can't compare it to anything else. Terry Allen said, "You don't know if you're in the center of the universe or if you're just this little speck in the middle of this vast nothingness." I don't know, either, but I just love it.

{ N e a l   M c C o y }

One of the friendliest guys in country music, Neal McCoy is rarely in a bad mood. "I've got a lot of wrinkles, but I think it's from smiling too much!" he says with a twinkle in his eye. A self-proclaimed "Texapino"—his father is a Texan of Irish descent, and his mother is Filipino—Neal has a kinetic energy that makes every performance unforgettable. Known for taking the stage without a set list and sometimes being known to climb on rafters, Neal gives new meaning to the word "entertainer." Despite having three platinum albums to his name, he is still a man of simple tastes. Give him a pair of Wranglers and a cheeseburger with mayonnaise, and he's ready to hit the road. When he's not on tour with his family in tow, this rich baritone can be found working with the East Texas Angel Network, a foundation he and his wife, Melinda, established twelve years ago to help the families of children with life-threatening diseases. But his good deeds don't stop there—he counts his several USO tours to Iraq and Afghanistan as some of the most rewarding moments in his career.

My singing aspirations were solidified one night when I was ten years old. Sitting in front of the television watching *American Bandstand*, I saw the Jackson 5 run onstage to thunderous applause. Michael was dancing around and singing, "ABC, easy as One, two, three . . ." I thought to myself, *Golly, here I am the same age as that kid and he gets to do that.* I don't know if it was actually the music or getting out of school and chores that appealed to me, but I knew it was great. Singing and dancing looked like far more fun than chores and homework. *That's what I need to do with my life,* I thought.

Rodeo time in Jacksonville was another highlight of my childhood. Anytime the rodeo came to town, I was the happiest kid around. It ran for four nights a year, and I was there every night. During the day, I hung out by the chutes watching the cowboys run the bulls in the pen. I was a smooth talker, so I tried to offer whatever help I could. Every now and then they let me bring water. Then I'd make my move and try to bargain my way into the rodeo that night. The cowboys were great, but the best part of the rodeo was the singers. I'd climb onto the fence line and marvel at them up onstage. Seeing superstars like Eddy Arnold and Michael Landon come to a little bitty town just opened my eyes right up. *Man, that's cool,* I thought to myself.

It would be years and years before my dreams came true. But they did, more than I ever thought they would. I was even invited to a state dinner at the White House! What a fantastic night. Of course, it was a little overwhelming since my wife and I had never been to a highfalutin party like that before. I was seated at a table with six other people including President Bush and Justice Sandra Day O'Connor. When dinner was served, I was a little confused about which silverware to use. There were so many utensils, glasses, and plates. I had no idea where to start. Justice O'Connor, being a country girl herself, leaned in and graciously told me, "Start at the outside and work your way in." We had a good laugh, and once we figured out which wineglass was mine, the rest of the night went smoothly. Not bad for a boy from the country, but then again, the main guy at the table was, too.

Eddie Montgomery

Eddie Montgomery doesn't remember a time without music. Playing in his family band and hanging out in honky-tonks when most kids his age were in bed, Eddie got a crash course in life as a musician. Soon he formed the band Young Country with his brother John Michael and his fellow Kentucky native Troy Gentry. After John Michael scored a solo record deal, the other two teamed up to form Montgomery Gentry. When they hit the Lexington club circuit with their raw songs about the highs and lows of real living, the powerhouse duo's buzz quickly spread across the country. Their rare ability to blur the lines between life and music has struck a nerve with legions of devoted fans. In 2000, they won a Country Music Association Vocal Duo of the Year Award and the American Music Award for Favorite New Artist—Country. After selling millions of records, the pair released a greatest-hits album titled *Something to Be Proud Of* in 2005.

I grew up in a one-stoplight town. Although, to be entirely honest it was more like I grew up in a few different one-stoplight towns, because when your family plays music, you move around quite a bit. Instead of living room furniture, we had music equipment. Guitar amps and drum thrones were the chairs in my house. Mom was a drummer, Dad was a guitar player, and the bartenders were our babysitters. We couldn't afford real babysitters, so our parents just took us with them everywhere. It wasn't until I was older that I realized we were poor. I remember Mom cussing out the utilities guy for cutting our electricity, which happened quite often. Of course, he was just doing his job, but she had three kids, and electricity was a necessity. I reckon it was because of the music that we always had food on the table—soup, beans, and fried potatoes most of the time. The music never let us know we were poor.

I was basically born with an instrument in my hand. My old man always told me that music's the worst drug in the world because there is no cure for it. Once it's in your blood, it's in your blood. He was right. Music has never been a job for me. It's been my soul. It was never about picking up girls, and I damn sure didn't do it for the money. I got into it because I loved it. And I found guys to play with who loved it as much as I did. If we weren't playing somewhere, we were going to a bar to sit in with somebody to jam and play, or we would find our way to playing at somebody's house. It was what we did all the time. Like my dad said, "If you want to get there and you want to make it, you got to eat it, breathe it, and sleep it." So that's what we did.

A lot of our music comes from the stories I listened to during my childhood. It's about people coming into the bars, whether for the first or the hundredth time, whether they were coming in to celebrate or coming in with a broken heart. It's about everyday life—the good, the bad, the ugly, and the party on the weekend. With us, what you see is what you get. We're not perfect. We don't sing perfect every night. We probably don't play perfect every time. Sometimes we raise too much hell. But we're always going to have fun.

Growing up country—there's nothing like it. It's growing up with your grandmother and granddaddy around; it's getting your ass whipped when you need it; it's a lot of love when you need it, great cooking in the kitchen, and always being real. When I was cutting tobacco for a nickel a stick and baling hay for hours on end, I couldn't wait to get off that damn farm. But once I got off it, I couldn't wait to get back. Man, that's who I am. I don't always say the right thing, but I always say what's in my heart.

Darrell Waltrip

Not one to stand on the sidelines, Darrell Waltrip jumped into a go-kart when he was twelve years old and never looked back. As a professional who thrived on competition, Darrell made a splash with his performance both on and off the track. His aggressive driving style led an opponent to nick-name him "Jaws" after a particularly grueling and cutthroat race. In his usual good-natured, competitive spirit—or what he calls "co-opetition"—Darrell confidently strutted onto the track the following day and displayed an inflatable shark in his pit. Among his prestigious racing honors are three Nextel Cup titles, the 1989 Daytona 500, the 1992 Southern 500, and an un-precedented five Coca-Cola 600 titles. His eighty-four Winston Cup race wins are the most by any driver in NASCAR's modern schedule format, and he is the only driver to win $500,000 or more in a season eighteen times. A three-time National Motorsports Press Association Driver of the Year winner, Darrell was named NASCAR's Driver of the Decade for the 1980s.

I spent my childhood summers in a Pepsi-Cola truck. My dad drove one—he was a route salesman, and I helped him when-ever I wasn't in school. One day—it turned out to be a fateful day—we went to West End Hardware. Right in front of the store the guys were unloading go-karts from a truck, and I was hooked.

I was twelve years old, and I had a vision of someday racing at Daytona.

"Dad, I think I'd like to drive one of those," I said. But it wasn't that easy. See, there were five kids in my family. When your dad drives a truck and your mom is a cashier at the IGA, it takes everything just to keep the family clothed and fed. A four-hundred-dollar go-kart isn't at the top of the list. It may as well have been two million dollars. We'd go by that hardware store twice a week on the route, and every time I'd get out of the Pepsi truck and sit in that go-kart, dreaming of driving it as fast as I could.

One day the owner of the store said to my dad, "Look, we're going to race 'em. We're going to take three of these things up to the shopping center parking lot this Sunday and let people drive them. Why don't y'all come up there Sunday and take one around and see how you like it?" I couldn't even sleep for the next few days. I was just jumping up and down. I couldn't wait to get to that parking lot.

Finally Sunday arrived. At 7:00 a.m. we were there. I was so excited I could hardly stand myself. I got on that thing, and it was like I'd been driving one my whole life. I just hopped on it and I took off, running wide open around this racetrack. I was faster than everybody out there, but what sealed the deal was that Dad went out there and drove one, too. He thought it was pretty cool. The next week when we went to the hardware store, the owner said, "Look, I'll sell you one of these on credit. If you can pay some money down now and some every month, I'll let you have it. This kid needs a go-kart. He's really good, I think he's got some potential."

We took it home that day. It was orange, like the color of Tony Stewart's car. My first number was 103. I was so happy. But here's the thing: we had no idea how much it would take to keep it going. I must have burned up a set of tires every weekend, plus the gas and all the maintenance—it was more than my dad had bargained for. But we were addicted, so every Sunday we'd throw that go-kart into the trunk and take it to a race. Some fathers go hunting and fishing to bond with their sons. For us, it was the go-kart races.

Fast-forward to the best win of my life: 1975, Mother's Day weekend, Nashville, Tennessee. It was my first win in the Cup Series. I've got pictures of the whole family in Victory Circle. My family sacrificed a lot early on for me to be able to do what I wanted to do. Those sacrifices, fortunately, ended up paying dividends to all of us. There were times when it didn't seem like it would, but it has turned out better than any of us could ever have hoped.

FAMILY

{ **Carl Acuff Jr.** }

With the last name Acuff, you can be sure you'd grow up with a healthy knowledge of your country roots. Carl Acuff Jr. certainly did. He has had big shoes to fill being from the Roy Acuff family. Roy, of course, was known as the King of the Grand Ole Opry, and though Carl never met him, he has been blessed to be around people who have told many wonderful stories about Roy. With music running in his blood, Carl released his debut album to independent country radio, where it quickly scored three Top 40 independent singles. While proud to preserve his traditional country roots, Carl also mixes in his love of good ol' rock and roll when he hits the road. Logging countless miles during his fourteen years on tour, Carl has entertained thousands of fans with his high-energy shows night after night.

From my earliest memories I remember hearing my dad playing music. My sister and I watched *Hee Haw* on Saturday nights as Dad and his band headed out to a honky-tonk to play the songs we had heard on the show. I always wanted to go along and I knew in the back of my mind that someday that was what I would be doing. Although Dad started out playing 1950s and 1960s rock and roll, by the time we came along his song list included people like Freddie Hart, Johnny Rodriguez, Merle Haggard, Buck Owens, Waylon, Willie, Charlie Daniels, and Joe Stampley. Dad,

John Criner, and Billy Evans practiced right there in our living room. I watched Billy, who played drums, closely. I got my first set when I was about three years old. By the time I was twelve, I had watched enough, and I finally played my first paying gig. It was a wedding anniversary with a big band and I was the second drummer onstage. It was great, just as I thought it would be, and from that moment on, I was hooked.

I've devoted my life to making music, and though it's been hard at times, there's nothing else I'd rather be doing. Over the last fourteen years I've worked with most of the people that I grew up watching on *Hee Haw* and listening to on the *Grand Ole Opry*. I've taken my show to forty-six states and traveled almost two million miles performing for thousands of fans. As much as I love the country music industry, I still place family above all else. Being onstage is an incredible feeling, but spending time with my family just can't be beat.

I was blessed to have all of my grandparents until I was grown. Along with my parents, they taught me to milk cows, slop pigs, grow a garden, and hunt and fish—all the things a country boy needs to survive. I still love to garden and hunt, and there's nothing I like better than to load up my family, throw a tent and a couple of sleeping bags in the truck, drive down to the woods, and camp. With our fishing poles, we sit down on a creek bank and watch the sunset. Life doesn't get much better. And if we catch a fish, that's just a bonus.

After all these years of traveling this great country, I have settled with my wife, Nina, and our son, Carl III, only twenty miles from where I started. I live in the little town of Everton, Arkansas, with a population of 170 people. It's a great place to give my kids the same country upbringing I received.

Senator Lamar Alexander

A seventh-generation Tennessean, Senator Lamar Alexander was born to a kindergarten teacher and elementary school principal. His interest in politics was sparked at just ten years old, when his father took him to the Blount County Courthouse to meet Howard H. Baker, their local congressman. The young boy from Maryville was sure he'd just met the most respected man in the world, other than his father and his preacher, of course. During the 1978 campaign for governor of Tennessee, he made a name for himself by walking across the state—a thousand miles—wearing a now-famous red and black plaid shirt. He won that election and went on to make history by being the first person reelected to a second four-year term in 1982. After his second term was up, he and his family took an adventurous step out of the public spotlight by moving to Australia for six months. In 2002, he made a triumphant return to politics with his election to the U.S. Senate. The only Tennessean to be popularly elected both governor and U.S. senator, he chairs the Senate Education and Early Childhood Development Subcommittee and is a member of the Foreign Relations and Budget committees. A classical and country pianist and the author of seven books, including *Six Months Off*, which is the story of his family's move Down Under, Senator Alexander helped Tennessee become the third-largest auto producer and the first state to pay teachers more for teaching well.

I grew up on Ruth Street in Maryville, Tennessee, near the Great Smoky Mountains. Ruth Street runs from the Blount County Fire Hall on Broadway to Pistol Creek at the bottom of the hill. The fire hall was the best place for lobbing snowballs at the tourists passing through on their way to Florida. Almost always when they stopped, they would roll down their windows and scream in some unusual accent, "You blasted little hillbillies. You've hit my windshield!" We were and we had.

By the time I was ten, my alarm clock was set to ring at four each morning. In the dark, I got dressed, tossed a newspaper bag over my bike, and raced to the Broadway Food Market. There I picked up a packet of about seventy-five *Knoxville Journal*s, threw them into my bicycle basket, and was on my way. With one hand I could fold and pitch a *Journal*—always on the porches, never in the yards—and steer with the other hand.

At 5:00 a.m. I was back in bed. I was up again at six to practice the piano because I liked it, because it left the afternoons free for sports, and because I had to. While Mother's kitchen produced smells of bacon and the strong coffee that Dad liked, I sat in the next room at our thirdhand upright Kimball piano that Mother had bought with her schoolteacher's savings. My piano lessons began when I was three and stopped when I enrolled at Vanderbilt University when I was eighteen. Piano playing was how my mother interpreted for me the first catechism of the Presbyterian Church. She would say, "Man's chief end is to glorify God, so the reason you play music so beautifully is because God gave you that gift."

One of Mother's gifts was handing down her Rules of Life, something she had apparently inherited from her father, R. R. Rankin. In pronouncing these Rules, she had a habit of improvising too much. For example, on sunny October afternoons—when the neighbors' burning leaf piles scented the air—Mother would rule, "God gave us this beautiful day to rake leaves." Such rulings led me also to see God as responsible for making the hedge grow high, so I could cut it, and for making the white paint peel off our frame house, so I could paint it. I did not argue with either Mother or God, but I thought one or the other or both were taking unfair advantage of their positions.

Dealing with these extra Rules—and playing side-yard football and softball—kept my afternoons busy and full until five-thirty, when I would rush to the Broadway Food Market for my package of afternoon *News Sentinel*s. While it was still daylight, I could run the Ruth Street route in half the time it took to deliver the morning *Journal*s and arrive home just in time for supper at six. Then, by six-thirty on Monday, Wednesday, and Friday evenings, Dad and I would be flopped on the floor in the living room in front of the tall mahogany Zenith radio, eager for the staccato trumpet that announced the beginning of another adventure of *The Lone Ranger*. On warm autumn Saturday afternoons we'd carry the radio to the front porch and turn it up so we could hear University of Tennessee football games while we worked in the yard. Bringing our radio outside always seemed to me a waste of time because everyone else on Ruth Street had their radios outside, too, turned up so loud that we could have heard the game anyway.

Our New Providence Presbyterian Church was the center of a good part of our lives. In addition to Sunday school, church, and choir on Sunday, there was Fellowship on Sunday night, Boy Scouts on Monday night, choir practice on Tuesday, prayer meeting on Wednesday, weekend rallies and vacation school and church camp in the summer.

I walked every day to West Side Elementary School (where my father had been principal until he took a job at the Alcoa aluminum plant to support the family better). There I received a vigorous education as well as 105 black marks in Mrs. Jackson's fourth grade (5 black marks meant you were in serious trouble), for which I was given two licks with the paddle. The paddling smashed two Milky Way candy bars in my back jeans pocket, to the delight of the eagerly witnessing class. The next morning during first-period class, when each of us said out loud a one-sentence prayer, my classmate Bill Earnest's sentence was "Dear God, please forgive Lamar Alexander for all his sins."

When I got in trouble at school, I got in trouble at home, which is the way things used to work. My teachers taught me the importance of the Pledge of Allegiance, of telling the truth, of the greatness of this country and of our civilization, of the value of working hard and being on time, and of the difference between right and wrong.

Dad kept his finances to himself, but it was clear he never had money to waste. We had no car until I was ten, and when we got it—a white 1940 two-door Chevy—a couple of my classmates, whose fathers had newer and bigger cars, smirked. But nobody in Maryville smirked much because it was hard to tell who was poor and who was rich. Most people had some money because of the thousands of jobs for aluminum workers at the Alcoa plant, or because of farming, or both. But people who were rich, relatively speaking, were careful not to act rich, and most people who were poor did their best neither to feel nor to act poor.

Probably the thing that stirred up my dad the most was when Eleanor Roosevelt, and then Lyndon B. Johnson, pronounced us Appalachian poor. Talking about this so upset Dad that the veins in his throat would swell and turn blue. This was because Eleanor

Roosevelt and Lyndon B. Johnson were Democrats, and we were Republicans. Dad practiced his Republicanism the way I practiced the piano, systematically—he practiced it over coffee at Byrne Drugstore, in the courthouse on Saturday mornings, and as a member of the local Republican Party executive committee.

My best summers as a teenager were spent on my grandparents' farm in the southwest corner of Missouri—enjoying the fresh taste of raw milk and butter every day, scything grass beneath the hot Missouri sun, and helping Granddad type up the genealogical records of his Scotch-Irish ancestors way back to 1688 in County Derry, Ireland.

Granddad's correspondence with relatives helped to found the Rankin reunions at Mount Horeb Presbyterian Church in Dumplin Valley in Jefferson County, where our ancestors settled in 1783, thirteen years before Tennessee became the sixteenth state. Sometimes at those reunion services I played the old upright piano while relatives sang "God Be with You till We Meet Again," which was written by Jeremiah Rankin in 1880. After a covered-dish dinner-on-the-grounds of fresh yellow corn, red tomatoes, fried chicken, and biscuits, we would follow Granddad behind the church toward a row of gravestones. As in every mountain graveyard, all the stones still standing faced east (because the Bible teaches that Jesus will come again from the East and no family wants its loved ones facing the wrong way when he comes). Granddad would pause for silence, and then, looking down at us children, intone: "I am the fifth, your mother standing here is the sixth, you are the seventh, and your children will be the eighth generation. No one except the Cherokees goes further back than that in east Tennessee."

When Grandmother died in 1967, Granddad sold his farm in Missouri and moved back to east Tennessee into a little house on

Ruth Street. "You can't take the mountains out of a mountain boy," he pronounced—another Rule of Life he passed down to us. In one of our last front-porch conversations on Ruth Street, Granddad asked me, "Well, what are you going to do, Lamar?" "Maybe someday run for governor," I answered. "I wouldn't," he said. "Politics is too hard. But if you do, aim for the top. There's more room there."

Keith Anderson

When a shoulder injury ended his pursuit of a career in professional base-ball, Keith Anderson didn't hesitate for a second. He turned all of his atten-tion to the other love in his life—music. He emptied his bank account, packed up his less than reliable car, and moved to Nashville. "Whatever I set my mind to do, I believe I can do" is the credo he lives his life by. Working as a waiter on Music Row, Keith (with his demo CD burning a hole in his pocket) was constantly meeting music industry people, but it was playing in a flag football game with the songwriter George Ducas that ended up leading to his first break. The two hit it off and were soon collaborat-ing on songs. Keith quickly found success as a songwriter, racking up the Grammy-, Country Music Association-, and Academy of Country Music–nominated "Beer Run," a hit duet recorded by Garth Brooks and George Jones, as well as "The Bed," which appeared on Gretchen Wilson's 2004 debut album. Dubbed by *Music Row* magazine as an "industrial-sized hunk," Keith turned his attention to performing his own music in 2005 with the release of his album, *Three Chord Country and American Rock & Roll.*

If you ever find yourself in a little town off I-44 in Oklahoma with a sign that says, "Welcome to Miami," whatever you do, *don't* pronounce it like the city in Florida. You'll get corrected real quick. It's "My-am-uh." Growing up, we were always told it was the correct Indian pronunciation, but I just think it's the way Oklahomans talk. Miami is where the kids from surrounding smaller towns come to "drag Main" on Friday and Saturday nights. Fill up with a tank of gas and a Coolie from QuikTrip and you're all set. Wind down Main Street till you get to Security Bank and Trust, turn around and do Main Street again until you hit Safeway, then just go back and forth till you hear whose parents are gone for the night. That's where you'll find the party.

We loved a good time. With three boys in the family, my dad, Leroy, had to break out the belt now and again. Well, maybe it was more like now and again and again and again. I think I still have "Leroy" imprinted backward on my ass today. I remember getting into some real trouble at the dinner table. Every night, the whole family ate together. We'd sit down, hold hands, and pray. We couldn't touch the food before the prayer was finished. Fortunately, when we were young, we used the quickest prayer we could spit out—"God is great and God is good, Let us thank him for our food. Amen!" Anyway, back then I hated vegetables. I mean, just *hated* them. But I wasn't excused from the table until they were gone. So I had the bright idea to hide them in my drinking glass. Very quickly, I scooped them up and dropped them in my cup, over and over until my plate was cleared right off. Thinking I'd eaten up all my greens, my parents excused me from the table. I was on my way to play with my brothers when suddenly I heard my mom's voice, "Keith, get back to the table right now!" Uh-oh. Mom had discovered the contraband while she was washing the dishes. I hadn't thought out my disappearing-peas plan past the getting-excused-from-the-table stage.

Food was at the heart of our home. And, other than those troublesome vegetables, I loved all of it. We fried everything— we'd have even fried the water if we could've. When people meet me, they think I'm big, but compared with my family, I'm the runt.

I've got family members coming in at over three and four hundred pounds—you've got to learn how to hold your own during a big hug or you just won't survive. Our family get-togethers are one huge smorgasbord of polyester muumuus and fried food. Everyone loves to eat, cook, and fry so much we even have our own Anderson Family Cookbook. Food and family, doesn't get much better than that.

Tracy Byrd

Thanks to a fateful trip to the mall, where he was coaxed into singing Hank Williams's "Your Cheatin' Heart" in a little recording studio, the Texan Tracy Byrd discovered he loved singing. And, thankfully, he was good at it. The studio's owner knew talent when he saw it and immediately entered Tracy in a local contest. The smooth, rich baritone found his calling and hit Beaumont's club circuit with a feverish intensity. He scored the first of his thirteen Top 10 hits with "Holdin' Heaven" and struck a double-platinum success with *No Ordinary Man*. Byrd's heart is as big as his state, and his annual Tracy Byrd Homecoming Weekend event has raised over a million dollars for Children's Miracle Network, his charity of choice. And although music is his first love, he is an avid outdoorsman and for the second year running is the honorary chairman for National Hunting and Fishing Day.

I called her Nana. She was my mom's mom, and as far back as I can remember, she was different from other grandmas. My grandpa passed away when I was a baby, so Nana was on her own. She was beautiful, but she was tough—a true mountain woman. She lived five miles up the road from us, and I spent every free minute I had with her.

Summers were the best. May was squirrel-hunting season, and we couldn't wait to get out in the woods. I'd spend the night at her house, and with the first rays of sunlight seeping through the window, I'd hear Nana singing, "Who do I, who do I, who do I love? Don't I love that Tracy Byrd?" She'd sing that over and over again and hug me until I woke up.

A wood-burning stove in the middle of the house would be keeping our breakfast of scrambled eggs warm. Nana always cooked up some extra for our favorite lunch of canned potted meat and egg sandwiches. To this day, I don't really know what potted meat is, and I don't think I want to, but it sure tasted good after a morning of hunting. After breakfast, she'd wrap up our sandwiches in tinfoil, stuff them in a sack, and fill a thermos with coffee. With her 12-gauge and my .410-gauge gun, we'd head off into the woods. Hours and hours we'd spend hunting. Then we'd sit down, feast on our lunch, and just talk. She always made me feel like I was the only kid in the world. It was just the best.

If we weren't hunting, we'd be keeping busy checking our trotlines. We'd probably have about three hundred hooks out. In a little twelve-foot johnboat, we'd go out in the water, collect what was on the lines, rebait them, and spend the rest of the day bass fishing. Once evening came, we'd check the lines again, haul our catch back to the house, and clean the fish. An expert in resourcefulness, Nana kept the fish guts and froze them to use on our steel traps in the wintertime. She taught me how to live off the land. It was an incredible way to grow up. In the springtime, she'd start her garden. With her mule and plow, we'd plant almost three acres. You name it, we had it in there—tomatoes, peppers, eggplants, peas, beans, and probably about six rows of sweet corn and okra. We'd eat all we could, and then take some to my parents and friends. Nana still had so much left over that we'd can it all in Mason jars.

Nana taught me so much. Thanks to all of our hunting and fishing days, I knew the outdoors like the back of my hand. She spent thirty years of her life taking me on adventures she knew I'd love. Finally, the year before she died, I got to take her on a new adventure. Turkeys don't roam around southeast Texas, so turkey hunting was one of the few things she'd never done. I took her hunting down in south Texas, and she got a turkey her first morning out. At seventy-one years of age, she still had it. Mavis Vaughn—my Nana—was a true mountain woman and the best grandma I could have wished for. I can't imagine my life without her.

Brenda Lee

At a tiny four feet nine inches, Brenda Lee stands tall in the music business. Known for her big voice, her vast roster of accomplishments, and a music catalog that spans rock and roll, R & B, pop, gospel, and country, Brenda has garnered worldwide record sales of more than 100 million. She began recording at age ten and had her first hit song, "Sweet Nothin's," at age fourteen, which was closely followed by hit after hit, including "I'm Sorry" and the now-classic "Rockin' Around the Christmas Tree." In the pop field, Brenda enjoyed chart-topping success in the 1970s and earned a Grammy nomination for "Johnny One Time." Next came a slew of Top 10 country hits in the 1980s that included "Big Four Poster Bed" and "Tell Me What It's Like." During her legendary career, Brenda has performed in some fifty-two foreign nations and has recorded international hits in six languages. Her list of awards and accomplishments spans decades and circles the globe, including a Royal Command Performance for Queen Elizabeth II. Brenda is a member of the Rockabilly Hall of Fame and is the only female to be a member of both the Rock and Roll Hall of Fame and the Country Music Hall of Fame.

I was born Brenda Mae Tarpley in the charity ward of Atlanta's Emory University Hospital. My childhood home was made of weathered clapboards. There wasn't any paint on the house, and the yard was mostly dirt. It had three rooms and an outhouse. You drew water out of the well, and the iceman would come by in a truck once a week with the ice. See, we had electricity, but we didn't have a refrigerator or anything like that. We had one common bedroom, and all us kids slept together on an old iron bed. We had a primitive fireplace in one room with a big iron grate, and that was our heat source. If you wanted to be cooler in the summertime, you just raised the windows and prayed for a breeze. You had a washtub, and you took a bath in that. You didn't stay up late at night and waste electricity; the day was sunup to sundown. But that's the way my parents had been brought up, so I don't remember "growing up country" as being any type of particular hardship. My remembrances are fond.

I remember on Saturday nights, we'd all listen to the *Grand Ole Opry* on our plastic, table-model radio that ran on a battery. Ball games, news reports, *Amos 'n' Andy*, and the *Opry*. Those were the favorites at our house. My grandmama Lucy Emma made the most beautiful dresses for my older sister and me. No matter that they were out of feed and flour sacks. To us, they looked like they'd come out of a fancy department store. Daddy made almost all our toys—slingshots, wooden cars and boats, and little whittled figures. And every Friday on payday, he brought home three pink Kits candy taffy, one for each of us children. We'd get oranges at Christmas, and a lot of the time for lunch we'd have grease sandwiches. And you know what? I actually liked them. Church was a big part of our life. That was our socializing. It was like going to a family reunion. Afterward, there were often long stay-overs at my cousins' houses, and big evening meals with kinfolks were common.

Looking back now, I can't believe that I didn't know we were poor, 'cause we really were. But I was happy; I had people around me who cared about me and loved me; I had all I needed.

Barbara Mandrell

Glamorous music superstar. Best-selling author. Television actress. Barbara Mandrell does it all. The quintessential superwoman, Barbara shines whether she is performing for millions or sitting around the kitchen table with her family. Over the past three decades, this beloved Texan has released over thirty albums and sent scores of songs for a ride up both the country and the pop charts. The list of her accolades seems endless. Two Grammys and two Country Music Association Entertainer of the Year Awards (the first artist ever to win in two consecutive years) are a tiny sampling of the over seventy-five major awards she has earned. Born into a musical family, young Barbara sang all the time and played any instrument she could, and by age ten she was performing on television. With her rare combination of steely determination and genuine kindness, Barbara quickly made a name for herself in the 1970s and soon became one of the most prominent names in music with multimillion record sales worldwide. Her rise to the top was beautifully told in her autobiography, *Get to the Heart: My Story*. The book struck a chord with readers and soared to the *New York Times* best-seller list, staying there for six months. In 1997, Barbara's life story premiered as a Movie of the Week on CBS.

My sisters, Louise and Irlene, and I had the best growing-up years due to the influence of my daddy and his side of the family, the Mandrells, and to my mother and her side of the family, the McGills. We were raised to realize that God, family, and America are the most important things in life. We were taught the value of respect, manners, and to say, "Yes, sir," "No, sir," "Yes, ma'am," "No, ma'am," "Please," and "Thank you," and to thank God for all our blessings.

Even simple memories are precious to me. I can't see or eat blackberries without remembering Grandma McGill. She made wonderful blackberry cobbler for us after we had gone out and enjoyed the childhood adventure of picking blackberries. My memories of her and all my family are treasures of mine that are as sweet as Grandma's blackberry cobbler.

FAITH

Jason Allen

When most high school kids were hanging out at movie theaters and ball games, Jason Allen was honing his craft in dance halls and honky-tonks. By the time this east Texan was eighteen, he was fronting touring bands and making frequent trips to Nashville, where he immersed himself in the crazy world of the music business. Frustrated with the slow progress he was making in the music capital, Jason decided there was only one thing to do—go back home, put his trust in God, and find his music destiny a different way. It proved to be the smartest thing he could've done. D Records, whose past roster included George Jones, George Strait, and Willie Nelson, had recently been revived, and Jason was its first new signing. A crowd-pleasing entertainer who fills the dance floor in seconds and adeptly slides a Lone Star Light beer bottle up and down his six-string, Jason has talents that extend beyond his ability as a performer. An award-winning music producer for his work on Texas Renegade's *3 a.m.*, Jason recently produced the album *Gospel Memories* by his father, Wesley Sligar. "Wouldn't It Be Nice," the title track of Jason's new album, was written with his sister Rickie and his late mother when he was just sixteen. The song, one of his most personal, is an ode to the simpler times of country living. In 2006, the multitalented musician was nominated for the My Texas Music Entertainer of the Year Award.

grew up all over Texas. Wherever there was work, that's where we'd go. My dad and two older brothers were bricklayers, so we were at the mercy of where the next paycheck would come from. I'm the youngest of five, and by the time I was around, my brothers and sisters already had their own kids. About half the time, we all lived together. The old country lyric "Love grows best in little houses" sure is the truth. We always stuck together—I couldn't wait to get home from school to hang out with my parents. I'd go everywhere with them in our old pickup truck—just traveling, wherever the work was.

My dad would come home from work to get me and my mom: "Y'all get in the truck—we're going to the beer joint." That was our fun time. They'd have a beer, and I'd shoot pool and play the jukebox. Of course, sometimes the place would get a little rowdy, and my dad would say, "C'mon, y'all, we gotta go, it's getting kind of drunk in here." Traveling around with my mom and dad was the best education I could have asked for. I learned more from them than I ever did in school.

Of course, times could be hard. When I was in kindergarten, we lived on the river in Trinity, Texas, in an Army tent. My dad moved us there because he found work, but we didn't have a place to live, so we just headed for the campground. After a few months, my dad moved us into a little camper trailer. Boy, we were high-class at that point. We fished in the morning, and whatever we caught was our food for the day. Mama would cook our catch with potatoes and onions and throw in some weenies and beans, and we were good to go. I loved her cooking. Later, my dad landed a great job as a contractor in another town, and all the people there thought we were rich. So I went from being a poor little river rat to what the other kids in school thought was a snooty rich kid. Bankruptcy hit a few years later, and his business went under, so we headed back down to the water. We always went back to where the fish were because we knew we'd never go hungry.

Even when my parents were struggling to make ends meet, I never knew it. Some of my happiest memories are of when we lived down by the river. I remember getting my first guitar when I was five—sitting there watching Mama string it for me. We formed my first band when I was thirteen and named it Jason Allen and the Cross Stars. With my sister Rickie on tambourine and backup vocals and some other musicians thrown in the mix, we performed all over the place when I was in school. When I was fourteen, we landed a gig at the Virginia State Fair. Thanks to the rain outside, the tent we were performing in was jam-packed. I was pretty nervous, but Rickie kept telling me everything would be fine. To make matters worse, our guitarist didn't show up. My nerves were getting the better of me when my dad pulled me aside. "You need to just get up on there and play lead—just figure it out," he said. So I jumped up onstage and started rocking on guitar. I don't know where it came from. I guess the Lord just kind of dumped it in my lap—the whole place, all these people that came in from the rain, and the talent. I was playing lead guitar like it was second nature. The crowd just went crazy, and I remember having this rush and thinking, *This is it. This is what I was born to do, right here.* Bad weather, good family, and the Lord got it all started.

David Ball

Raised by a musical family, David Ball persuaded his parents to buy him his first guitar—a Stella. By the time he was in the seventh grade, David was holed up in his room writing songs. But the precocious musician needed a place to play, so he put together a band, named it the Strangers, and made a splash on the stage of his school's talent shows. After high school, David headed to Nashville with a couple of hometown buddies, but a year of sleeping on floors and splitting twenty bucks three ways a night was enough. Performing as Uncle Walt's Band, the trio packed up and moved to Austin, where they found crowds packing the dance halls and calling for encores. Living above a liquor store on Sixth Street and paying seventy-five dollars a month in rent, David ate, drank, slept, and breathed the vibrant music scene. Three successful albums later, the band broke up, and David decided to try his luck again in the music capital. The second time around proved to be the ticket. His 1994 album *Thinkin' Problem* went double platinum and garnered three hit singles. *USA Today* dubbed the album the "country debut of the year," and prestigious award nominations came flooding in, including a Grammy nod for Male Vocalist of the Year. The smooth-singing honky-tonker released his latest album, *Freewheeler*, in 2004.

I grew up in South Carolina in a big family—and there was always music. I guess my first memories are of my mother playing the piano. She was always willing to entertain us with a song. My father was a Baptist minister, so our lives were centered on the church. Get on your best clothes Sunday morning, sing some hymns, listen to the sermon (most of it!), sing some more, then home for a big dinner. Amen.

As a child growing up in upstate New York, Brian Prout first performed with his sister Lori during a song-and-dance routine. He grew up playing drums in various New York rock groups, but eventually found himself wanting to head south to make his way as a musician. In 1986, he became the drummer for Diamond Rio. The band's 1991 self-titled debut album contained its No. 1 single, "Meet in the Middle." Over the course of the band's career, they've had eight additional No. 1 singles, garnered three platinum and five gold records, and were inducted into the Grand Ole Opry in 1998. The group, which released its second greatest-hits album in 2006, is also a force in the world of philanthropy. For their tireless efforts on behalf of Big Brothers Big Sisters of America, as well as their years hosting the Arby's Charity Tour Nashville golf tournament and pounding the pavement as Team Rio in fundraising half marathons, Diamond Rio was honored with the prestigious Minnie Pearl Humanitarian Award in 2004. Prout now makes his home in Nashville with his wife and three children.

The pasture my friends and I used to hit golf balls in while avoiding the cow patties is now the back side and parking lot of a Wal-Mart superstore. We were only five miles outside Troy, New York, but back then it was like living in the boonies. Dairy farms surrounded us, with barbed-wire fence and cattle for as far as my eye could see. We lived out in the country, but every day after school I took the bus into downtown to work at my father's grocery store.

There were rough times. Dad was an alcoholic. I knew to steer clear of him occasionally, but he always put food on the table and a roof over our heads. And he instilled in me a work ethic that has driven me to where I am today. Luckily, I have a wonderful mother who told me it was her job to give me roots and wings. She gave me roots by grounding me in a value system I still live by. Faith. Family. Profession. If you follow the first one, the other two will naturally fall into place. And she gave me wings that empowered me to find my own path in life.

Of course, it took a lot of trial and error before I realized how powerful my mother's gifts were. I was living down in Florida and playing music six nights a week until three o'clock in the morning. For a single guy in his twenties, I thought I had it made. At least for a while. The scene got to be too crazy, and it was starting to catch up with me. Too much drinking, too much partying—I was starting to feel out of control and my self-respect was starting to suffer. One morning—it must have been about seven-thirty—I was on my way home from a post-gig party. I felt burned out and like I'd lost my direction in life. I'd just found out my dad was gravely ill—on his deathbed—but I didn't have enough money to get home. Suddenly I passed a little church on the side of the road. A guy was climbing down the ladder that was leaning against the marquee. He'd just finished hanging up the last letter of the latest inspirational message. I pulled up to the stoplight outside the church and glanced over to see: "Would the Boy You Were Be Proud of the Man You Are?"

Right then and there, I had an epiphany. I sat there and cried like a baby. *No way*, I thought to myself. *I was raised better than this.* Two weeks later, my dad passed away. I went to New York for the funeral and spent some time with my family. By the time I returned to Florida, my band had decided to go in a different direction. I was back to square one, flat broke, and by myself. But I kept repeating that question over and over in my mind. I decided to get my life going. I decided to be the man I knew I could be. It was then that I discovered the strength of the roots my mother gave me. And it was then that I found my wings.

K i m b e r l y   R o a d s

When you look up the definition of "persistence" in the dictionary, you should find the phrase "Little Big Town." Over the past seven years, the foursome have suffered frustrating and devastating setbacks in both their personal and their professional lives, fundamental life challenges that would have been too much for most groups to handle. But Little Big Town is more than just a group. They are like a family, and they found strength by leaning on each other. "We've been through so many storms that I have to believe that it's all been for a reason," says Kimberly Roads in her sweet-as-molasses Southern drawl. As a little girl growing up in the mountains of Cornelia, Georgia, Kimberly always knew she wanted to be a singer. When she enrolled at Samford University, the seeds of Little Big Town were planted. As a music major, Kimberly took advantage of every opportunity to sing. She met her future bandmate Karen Fairchild, and the two instantly clicked, both as friends and as musicians. Once they made the move to Nashville, they added Jimi Westbrook and Phillip Sweet to the mix, and Little Big Town was off and running. After they signed with Clint Black's Equity Music Group and released 2005's *The Road to Here* to great critical and popular acclaim, it was nothing but bright skies ahead for the band that never gave up.

O n lazy, hot Sunday afternoons in the summer, families got together to make homemade ice cream. We took turns sitting on the churn as the grown-ups cranked away at it. We each took turns sitting on a newspaper laid across the top of the cooler, and as soon as your rear end got cold, you knew it was someone else's turn to jump on. If we weren't hanging out by the ice cream maker, we were lying at the top of the bank and rolling ourselves all the way down. That was better done *before* we feasted on ice cream. We'd have cool, creamy vanilla ice cream with warm Hershey's chocolate syrup drizzled on top, and it was simply delicious.

My family's week revolved around the church. Every time those big doors opened, there we were. Mama played the organ while Daddy, who was the deacon, directed the choir. When I was eleven, the church pianist left, so I replaced her, banging away on the keys until I learned how to play the hymns.

One of my favorite things was Christmastime. And not because of the presents—though I didn't mind them—but because of the live Nativity scene. I was always an angel, as all the little girls were. We dressed up in our angel costumes with wings and stood in the little barn out in the church's front yard. It was freezing cold, so under those little outfits we wore coats and scarves and gloves. We looked like chunky little angels. Mama was always Mary, and Daddy was always Joseph. One year, when my sister was a newborn, she was the baby Jesus. The newest baby in church was always baby Jesus. On Christmas Eve, we'd head home and warm ourselves up as Daddy read the scripture in Luke of the Christmas story. Gathered around his chair, we loved listening to him read to us. After we prayed together, Mama gave us all boxes with our new Christmas pajamas in them. Then it was off to bed in our matching pj's. It's such a beautiful tradition, and we still enjoy it year after year.

It is my faith that has given me unbelievable strength to get through the difficult times. When my husband passed away, I was devastated. It was a pain I didn't know how to get through. But I leaned on the foundation of my faith, and it gave me a new level of grace and mercy that I never knew existed before. I honestly don't know how I could have gone on without it. The faith that my small-town community was built on truly saved me. And it was those friends from my childhood who gave me solace. It had been years since I had spoken to many of them, but they gave me such support and love and comfort—it was like we had never been separated. It became so clear that in our small Southern town, we were taught to love and take care of one another.

Dana Williams

Born in Dayton, Ohio, and moving to Nashville at age eleven, Diamond Rio bassist Dana Williams was performing in church when he was seven years old. He listened to other genres of music growing up, but came back to country, the music he was raised on, when it came to playing his own. Williams was the final member of Diamond Rio to join the lineup in 1989. Over the course of the band's career, they've sold over ten million records worldwide and scored twenty-five Top 10 hits. In May 2006, the group released its second greatest-hits album. In recognition of their philanthropic efforts—hosting the Arby's Charity Tour Nashville golf tournament, serving for over a decade as national spokespeople for Big Brothers Big Sisters of America, running in fund-raising half marathons as Team Rio—Diamond Rio was honored with the Minnie Pearl Humanitarian Award in 2004.

I grew up in a family of devout Southern Baptists—in fact, I think we had our own key to the church. As a kid, I wasn't crazy about listening to the pastor's sermon, but I had to act like I was. If I was unlucky enough to fall asleep, even for a second, my granny would nearly pinch my arm completely off.

Mother ran a pretty strict household, so I kept myself in line. Most of the time. My daddy worked second shift at the McCall's printing factory, so he was gone from 2:30 to 11:30 at night. But my mother did just fine when it came to discipline. There was this imaginary line she set for me in the yard. It set the boundary of where I was allowed to play, but every single time I went out there, I'd try to go over that line. It got to the point where I'd walk to the line, look back at her, and stick my foot one inch onto the forbidden side. It took nine paddles before I finally looked at that line, turned around, and walked away.

My parents never allowed smoking or drinking in the house. Never, ever. One hot summer day I rode my bike to the store and bought a bottle of IBC root beer. It came in one of those old-fashioned bottles. I brought it home and put it in the fridge. A short time later, I heard my mother having an absolute fit in the kitchen. She poured it down the sink but didn't want to throw it in our trash, for fear that the trashmen would see the incriminating bottle. "Mother, it's just root beer," I pleaded. "Well," she replied, "it looks too close to the real thing, and there will be none of it in this household!" So much for root beer.

It may sound like my Southern Baptist upbringing was overly strict. But I was raised in a house full of love and good values. To this day, I've never had a drink. And to be honest, I don't think I've missed out on too much. The daily prayers we said before dinners during my childhood continue to be said by my own family today. Having God in my life and my family's life is nothing but a blessing that I will forever be thankful for.

HARD WORK

John Conlee

Plowing fields, slopping hogs, and harvesting grain—that's life out in Kentucky farm country. From the time he could walk, John Conlee was taught two valuable lessons: to work the land and to respect it even more. When he wasn't working on the family farm, John performed on local radio and in the barbershop quartet of his small town. As an adult, he became a licensed mortician, but his life path took a radical turn when he moved to Nashville and recorded a demo. With his distinctive melancholy voice, John scored his first hit in 1978 with "Rose Colored Glasses," which would become his signature song over the ensuing years. One of the most respected and prolific vocalists from the urban cowboy era, John has proved his staying power over and over with twenty-six singles making their mark in the Top 20, eight of which have reached the coveted No. 1 spot on the national country charts. Despite all his success, John is still a farm boy at heart. In between his touring on the road and his tireless work on behalf of Farm Aid, John's happiest times are spent with his family on their thirty-two-acre working farm outside Nashville. His latest album is 2006's *Country Heart*.

I was raised on a farm in Woodford County, Kentucky, about twenty miles from Lexington. I guess the farm life took, because we still operate that one and I live on another in the middle of Tennessee with my family.

My work ethic was established at an early age on the farm. Not only did we keep up with our own operation, but we also did custom machine work for other farmers in the area, which made each workday a double whammy. When you're not taking care of your own livestock and crops, you are baling hay, combining, or filling silos for neighbors. Over the years, we raised cattle, hogs, sheep, and chickens and kept workhorses and mules. We also raised tobacco, hay, and other feed crops along the way.

I spent the first days of spring riding a tobacco setter and the first days of winter in the tobacco stripping room. Those operations served as bookends for all the other field work between spring and summer, although there was still plenty to do through the winter, feeding livestock the hay we'd baled the summer before.

While there were times I was a little jealous of my city friends who had more time to play sports and hang out, I now count those long workdays as an irreplaceable blessing in my life. Farm life afforded me the opportunity to spend my free time at a pond fishing or in the woods with a .22 on my shoulder. Those quieter moments spent with nature were a much healthier influence than anything I could have done on urban streets. And hey . . . I got to drive tractors!

While living in the country and/or being a farmer holds no guarantee that a person will develop a high level of good old-fashioned common sense, I'm convinced it increases the odds considerably. I've often thought that if our politicians and national newspeople spent the majority of their time out here with us instead of huddled up together in Washington and New York, some of that common sense just might rub off on 'em. And I know they'd have a better picture of what America is really all about.

I'm thankful for many things in my life, and being raised in the country and being able to raise my kids on the farm are way up on my list. They are some of the best ways I can think of to observe the Lord at work.

Karen Fairchild

Traveling up a rocky road makes reaching the top that much sweeter. It's certainly true for Karen Fairchild and the rest of Little Big Town. The band was hit with hard knock after hard knock but defied the odds and broke into country music's elite with the release of the critically acclaimed 2005 album *The Road to Here*. Like her three bandmates, Karen got her musical start singing in her family church. After college, she moved to Nashville to launch her music career, where her friend and fellow musician Kimberly Roads soon joined her. During a brainstorming session on how to set themselves apart in Music City, the two friends with big dreams realized they needed to do something different. Something that had never before been done in country music. Try as they might, they couldn't think of any group made up of two girls and two guys. Just like that, their path became clear, and, with the addition of the singer-guitarists Jimi Westbrook and Phillip Sweet, Little Big Town was born.

Karen, we are going to miss you sooooo much! We love you! We just love you!" said my new friends. I had just moved to Georgia and was bombarded with hugs from a dozen fourteen-year-old girls at a church camp the summer before my ninth-grade year. I suddenly realized things were different in the South—this wouldn't have happened back in Indiana—and I loved it. My parents are true Southerners, but I was brought up in the Midwest. Despite our geographic location, my parents ran a household packed with Southern flavor. Family, community, and church were the focus of everything we did. Singing my first solo in church while my dad was leading the music, and eating my mom's fantastic fried chicken, delicious coconut cake, and legendary breakfasts of homemade biscuits, fried apples, eggs, and pancakes—I've heard my dad gained forty pounds during their first two years of marriage—it was true Southern living.

You know, I really should have been paying more attention when she was doing her cooking magic, but I was too busy playing sports out in the yard. Being the middle child, I was very competitive. My younger brother and I used to clock each other in the forty-yard dash, and we'd play touch football for hours on end with our dad. But the only way to keep the peace was for Dad to be the all-time quarterback while my brother, sister, and I took turns running different coverages and passing the ball. One time, when my brother was getting big enough to really inflict some pain, he tackled me just as I leaped across the touchdown tree line. He just laid me out, and I had to go to physical therapy for weeks to get my hamstring working again. But at least I scored. (Though to this day, he insists I did not cross that line.) After that infamous tackle, our football game days were over.

Those games might be the only thing I've ever quit. For as long as I can remember, my parents made us believe in ourselves. They had such confidence in what we could do, so we did, too. I wouldn't have been able to make it through the last twelve years in Nashville without that confidence. Going back to day jobs after we had record deals, singing on the weekends to pay the bills—those weren't good times. But even with all the ups and downs, our band never, ever thought about quitting. Of course, there were times when the hope started to fade away, but one of us was always there to pick the others up and keep on going. That sense of devoted community in my band is what the South gave me. Those girls at church camp were just like my family—such an affectionate spirit and welcoming hospitality—they just want to love on people. And I love them right back.

Janie Fricke

"All I ever wanted to do was sing," says Janie Fricke, an Indiana farm girl who grew up tending animals in the barn and soared to stardom as an internationally acclaimed recording artist. During her childhood, Janie sang in a little church up the road from the family farm and spent hours learning the guitar from her father and playing along with her mother at the piano. While in college, Janie literally sang for her supper, strolling into restaurants and bars and asking the owners if she could sing a song or two. Her tenacity and fearlessness paid off when she moved to Nashville and initially found success doing commercial jingles. Working as a session backing vocalist led to a number of hit duets with Johnny Duncan, and her first solo hit, "What're You Doing Tonight," made the country Top 40 in 1977. She continued to record duets with Duncan, as well as with Charlie Rich, throughout the rest of the 1970s, but the 1980s was when Janie made her mark on the country music landscape as a solo artist. With a jaw-dropping sixteen Top 10 singles to her name, seven of which hit the No. 1 spot, Janie more than earned her two Country Music Association Female Vocalist of the Year Awards. Releasing a live album in 2002 and an album of bluegrass remakes of her 1980s hits in 2004, Janie continues to tour and spends her treasured downtime at home with her husband and animals.

I grew up on a working family farm in South Whitley, Indiana. Our dairy farm was full of cattle and chickens; we all worked the fields and had to take care of our chores. We had a couple of horses and a barn full of cats. When I was little, I loved taking care of the litters of kittens. No animals were allowed in the house—Mother wouldn't allow it—so I used to head out to the barn to play with the newborn kittens. Josephine was a calico cat—she was one of my favorites. She must have had about twenty litters of kittens. I spent hours with her kittens, teaching them how to walk, nurturing them when they were sick, trying to be their friend. I was so attached to them I spent most of my days in that barn.

When I was a little older, I drove the tractor all over the farm, and one of my favorite times of the year was hay-baling season. Not because I liked the work, but because I used to ask my dad to hire the cutest guys from the high school basketball team to help out. That made baling hay much more tolerable.

I used to help my grandfather carry milk from the barn to the room where it was homogenized. It went into a huge vat, and then was picked up by the milkman. My grandfather was getting up in years, and I used to help him walk to the house after a long day of working on the farm. That's a unique thing about growing up in a rural area. You are with your family all day, all night, all weekend. You aren't running around town, putting on lipstick, shopping for shoes, going to the movies. You are working side by side with your parents, your grandparents, and your neighbors. It is a community based on a strong work ethic where everyone is striving to do the best they can. Sometimes it can be a struggle, since farming depends on the weather. You can lose an entire crop very quickly, so you've got to get out there and work when the weather is cooperating.

When you grow up that way, you learn certain standards and values very early in life. It doesn't matter if you are in the North, South, East, or West, when you are raised with your parents and grandparents in a traditional type of family setting, there are rules that you just don't break: be good to other people, help others who are in need, go to church on Sundays, get involved in your community.

Being raised in the country is a way of growing up. At an early age, you learn the meaning of self-reliance, and you don't shy away from hard work. I learned about sacrifice, and I learned what "no" meant. I learned that life is not about instant gratification. Growing up poor and needing, wanting, and learning how to earn what you wanted gave me strong values. It wasn't the easiest life, it was full of tough love, but it gave me the motivation, the drive, and the work ethic to go out in the world and achieve what I wanted.

{ Jim Glaser }

Raised on a twelve-hundred-acre ranch in the heart of Nebraska, Jim Glaser and his two brothers learned both music and farm life. The three brothers formed a trio, Tompall & the Glaser Brothers, that played in schools and theaters and performed on local radio and television shows. Marty Robbins, one of the most popular country musicians at the time, heard the brothers sing and signed them to a record deal. As members of the venerable Grand Ole Opry for fifteen years, the group racked up hit singles, including "Through the Eyes of Love" and "California Girl (and the Tennessee Square)." While the trio was honored with nearly every group award country music had to offer, including a *Billboard* award for being the most awarded group in country music at that time, Jim remained active as a songwriter, studio musician, and background vocalist, appearing on albums for many prominent artists, including Robbins and Johnny Cash. The Glaser brothers' Nashville studio was a headquarters of sorts for the Country Music Outlaw movement and was a favorite hangout for Waylon Jennings, Bobby Bare, and Billy Joe Shaver. After the family band split up, Glaser maintained an active solo career, scoring a No. 1 hit with "You're Gettin' to Me Again" and earning the 1984 Academy of Country Music's award for Top New Male Vocalist of the Year.

My paternal grandfather immigrated to America from Austria. He told us about the terrible storms they endured on the crossing before finally standing with his parents on the deck of their ship as it glided past the Statue of Liberty, into New York harbor, and on to Ellis Island. After a few years in Wisconsin the family settled in central Nebraska, where Grandpa Glaser homesteaded and raised his family. My father, Louis, bought the land from his father, and there, with his wife, Marie, brought six children into the world. I was the youngest.

My father and mother were the hardest-working people I've ever known. Part of it was the way they were raised, but it was also a legacy of the 1930s, when America's Great Depression—coupled with a severe drought—left scars on their hearts and minds they would carry for the rest of their lives. Year after year Dad had to borrow money from the bank to feed his family and buy the seeds they planted each spring, seeds that never even sprouted in the parched soil.

I wasn't old enough to have experienced those years, but I know that our family and the farm only survived because of the strength and faith of our parents. Some of my earliest memories are of working in the fields and listening as Dad talked for hours, trying to convey to his children some of the wisdom for which he and Mom had paid such a dear price.

The rains finally came back to the plains and the Depression ended, but Mother Nature never allowed us to relax for long without reminding us of her dark side. In November 1948, Nebraska was hit with the worst blizzard in a century. Dad watched the darkening sky that morning and, like the captain of the ship on which his father and grandparents had crossed the Atlantic, shouted orders to us as we battened down the hatches of our farm. By the time the storm hit, our animals were all safe in barnyard pens, and we were all snug and warm in the house, sitting down to one of Mom's wonderful suppers, cooked on the old woodstove.

The storm raged all night and all the next day, and when we

awoke the following morning, it was to a world of blue skies, bright sunshine, and a wonderland of snowdrifts as high as the house. The driving wind had packed the snow until it was so hard our cattle could walk on it, and where the drifts covered fences, the animals were able to wander out of their pens. Dad and my older brothers built temporary fences on top of the drifts, the posts held firmly in the icy snow. I remember singing as loudly as I could as I walked to school that morning, my voice thin and crisp in the cold, dry air. I felt like a giant as I walked on the tops of trees and stepped over telephone lines.

Music was always an important part of our lives. My father played guitar and, with his brother Martin playing fiddle, supplied music for neighborhood barn dances. Mom used to play the piano and sing for us, songs she'd learned as a girl. Then, one dry fall day, our house caught fire and burned to the ground, taking most of our personal possessions—including Mom's piano—with it.

I started playing guitar when I was seven years old. My brother Tom taught me a few chords, even though my hands were so small my fingers barely reached three of the six strings. By the time I was nine, we were doing public appearances.

I don't remember a time when we didn't know with certainty what our life's work would be. Dad and Mom knew it, too, but until we were ready, there was livestock to tend and fields to plant and harvest. Music was a thread weaving itself through our young minds, but the farm was still the fabric of our lives.

I sang whenever I could, riding a horse bareback over the sandhill pastures to check on the cattle or riding a tractor cultivating the fields of corn. In the evenings Tom and Chuck and I would go to our room at the back of the house and practice for hours. No one made us do it; we did it because music had already become our passion and our goal in life. It was all we ever thought about.

Dad did his best to prepare us for the life we had chosen. Acting as our first agent, he booked us at various venues around central Nebraska and even talked a television station in Hastings into giving us a weekly half-hour show, which ran for thirteen weeks. Ironically, television was such a new medium at the time that our family didn't yet own a TV set.

When we were a little older, Dad drove us 180 miles to Omaha, where we auditioned for the then-touring *Arthur Godfrey's Talent Scouts* show. It would be our first national television appearance.

But it was in 1957 that our father pulled off the coup that would launch our music careers and change our lives forever. He talked his way backstage at a Marty Robbins concert in Grand Island and asked the star to listen to his sons sing. Marty graciously agreed and, liking what he heard, immediately offered us a recording contract and a job touring with his show.

And so, in January 1958—two weeks after my twentieth birthday—my brothers and I left the farm and drove to Nashville, Tennessee, a thousand miles away. It was dark when we pulled in, and I remember staring wide-eyed at the Music City skyline sailing past the car's window, feeling like Grandpa Glaser must have felt arriving in New York harbor. His anticipation and excitement for the new life that lay ahead couldn't possibly have been greater than mine were that night.

But there would be storms ahead for us, too. Ours was not the quick trip to the top I'd envisioned, but years of struggle. It wasn't until 1970 that Tompall & the Glaser Brothers received the Country Music Association's Vocal Group of the Year Award and another fourteen years before I had a No. 1 record as a solo artist. Somewhere along the line I came to understand the passion and love that had motivated my parents to keep trying despite crushing disappointments. Whenever I felt like giving up, I'd find a place where I could sit quietly and close my eyes. Before long I would hear Dad's voice as plainly as if I were back in those Nebraska cornfields, listening as he talked of integrity, faith, strength of character, and the courage to never quit, no matter how hard the battle. And soon I'd be ready to try again.

Andy Griggs

Music can be the greatest source of comfort during life's darkest times. Andy Griggs knows about it all too well. Growing up in small-town Louisiana, he focused on sports while his older brother and father played music in local bands and church choirs. After the unexpected death of his father when Andy was just ten years old, he and his brother Mason found solace by listening to their dad's favorite Merle Haggard album. Tragedy again struck the family eight years later with the death of Mason. In mourning, Andy picked up the guitar and found some much needed consolation by stepping into his brother's place in his old band and becoming a youth minister at his local church. With a vague goal of making music for a living, Andy arrived in Nashville with no tape, no contacts, nothing. But he had his voice, and that was enough. He saw his first single, "You Won't Ever Be Lonely," from his debut album of the same name, hit No. 2 on the charts in 1999. "Tonight I Wanna Be Your Man," from his second album, *Freedom*, flew into the Top 10, and his most recent album, 2004's *This I Gotta See*, contains the hits "If Heaven" and "She Thinks She Needs Me."

Every Christmas Eve, we had a great big get-together at our little bitty country church. All the family was there. Heck, half of our whole town was family. It was the most special time of Christmas because Santa was there. You'd sit on his lap and whisper in his ear what you wanted. When you're a kid, that's bigger than life. On this particular Christmas Eve, I turned to whisper into Santa's ear, and I noticed that he had tobacco juice dribbling down his snow-white beard. Upon closer inspection, I realized his beard was made of cotton balls. I asked Santa about the brown liquid, and he just heartily laughed, "Heh, heh, heh." Suddenly I realized it wasn't Santa. It was my uncle Connie. Everybody in the whole state of Louisiana knew that Uncle Connie chewed tobacco and that he had that laugh. I told him I wasn't buying one bit of it, but he kept insisting that he was Santa Claus and that he had his reindeer right outside.

That night when my daddy tucked me into bed, he sensed that I was upset and asked me what was wrong. Usually, it's really hard to get a six-year-old to go to sleep on Christmas Eve, but I had the blues. My daddy asked, "Son, what's wrong?" I said, "I don't know if you know this, but I think Uncle Connie was dressed up as Santa Claus tonight." Daddy chuckled a little. "What gave it away?" he asked. I told him about the tobacco juice. He asked what that told me. "There's no such thing as Santa Claus," I said. Little did my daddy know that what he said next would stay with me for the rest of my life. "Son," he said, "there's a whole lot of Santa Clauses in life that you'll find out ain't real. Every time you turn around, you'll find a Santa Claus. It all starts right here, so get ready."

Now when I think about that fateful day, it's comical. Poor Uncle Connie, with that tobacco-stained beard just about ready to fall off. But what I remember the most is what my daddy said. I think the lesson that he wanted me to learn was not to take things at face value. There was no way that I could have fully understood his advice until I'd grown up. Life is full of mountaintops and valleys. You're bound to run into someone or something that will disappoint you. Every time that happens, I look up to heaven and say,

"Daddy, here's another Santa Claus." His words didn't make me cynical. In fact, I'm optimistic every time I look into someone's eyes. But it's not earth-shattering when somebody lets me down. His advice has proven to be invaluable to me, especially when it comes to my music career. There are a lot of times when I can look at Nashville and think there's nothing but Santa Clauses and the North Pole up there. But I just take everything in stride and try not to pay attention to anything but the music. Remembering his words keeps me strong and keeps me trekking through the valleys to get to the next mountaintop. That's a pretty good legacy to leave a six-year-old on Christmas Eve.

Buddy Jewell

Despite being rocketed to instant stardom in 2003 as the winner of the USA Network's first *Nashville Star* competition, Buddy Jewell is anything but an overnight success. His voice truly is a voice of experience. During his pre-fame years trying to break into the music business, Buddy performed in musical numbers at Six Flags over Texas, sang in numerous dance halls and honky-tonks, and appeared on *Star Search*, where his success made him confident enough to pack up and try his luck in Nashville. He spent ten years in Music City singing on thousands of demo tapes before he got his break on *Nashville Star*. When he sang "Help Pour Out the Rain," the impact on the national audience was immediate. In their fervor to find out more about the unknown singer and his unforgettable song, thousands simultaneously flocked to Buddy's little Web site, which promptly crashed and cost him six hundred dollars to repair. Needless to say, it was money he was happy to pay. Since winning the competition, Buddy has seen his debut album hit gold status as his wildly popular songs "Help Pour Out the Rain" and "Sweet Southern Comfort" sailed to the top of charts across the music industry. In 2005, Buddy again struck a chord with his fans. "If She Were Any Other Woman," a song from his second album, *Times Like These*, enjoyed an impressive twelve-week reign as the No. 1 selling country single. In recognition of his hard-won success, Buddy has been honored with nominations for a Grammy, the Academy of Country Music's Best New Artist Award, and the Country Music Association's Horizon Award.

rowing up, I spent hours down on the banks of the Mississippi River watching the tugboats push barges up to St. Louis and down to Memphis and New Orleans. In the summertime, I liked to sit outside at night to see hundreds of thousands of stars twinkling down at me from the skies above my hometown of Osceola, Arkansas. It was a simple way of life—if we turned our TV antenna *just so*, we could pick up the three channels broadcast out of Memphis.

It seems like my dad always worked two jobs. He had to since it took two or three to support our family. Thrashing beans, working in a factory, running a vending route—anything he could do to keep us afloat. My mom worked hard as well. She managed to raise us while working forty hours a week running the local bakery. We were typical lower-middle-class by my definition. Mom and Dad lived paycheck to paycheck, but we always had plenty to eat, nice clothes, and a solid roof over our heads. They really struggled, but I never had any idea. We always had wonderful birthdays and Christmas mornings. I never knew any different, so the tough times seemed normal to me. In fact, it wasn't until college that I realized you didn't have to mix water into every can of soup!

Even though my dad spent most of his waking hours working, he always managed to find time in his day for me. Any chance he got, he'd take me out to the yard to throw around a football or baseball. He could be really tough on me, and never, ever would he let me quit anything. If you started something, you finished it. Dad didn't believe in quitting, and he didn't believe in free rides. You had to earn everything you got in life. He also gave me the best advice I've ever heard: "Son, find a way to make a mark on this world, to make a difference in people's lives. It doesn't matter if it's big or small. Just find something you love to do, figure out a way to make a living at it, and make your mark out there."

Those words of wisdom helped get me through my first ten years in Nashville. When I arrived in the city, I took some pretty bad jobs to make ends meet. I worked selling cable TV door-to-door, hand washing and detailing cars, cleaning planes, and handling baggage at the airport. I did whatever I had to do during the day that would allow me to keep chasing my music dream at night. I wasn't afraid of hard work. I started mowing yards to earn spending money when I was only ten, and I'd spent my childhood watching my folks work hard. But there was one job that stood out from all the others as being the absolute worst: telemarketing. "Hey, Joe, how ya doin' today? Let me tell you about our brand-new customized baseball caps! They've got a picture of a '57 Chevy on them with 'Joe's Garage' blazing across the top in a rainbow arc. The detail on these babies is so spectacular you can almost see your face in the hubcaps! We're gonna give you a great deal—twelve dozen for $440. Can't go wrong with that. So, how you wanna pay for that? Cash, check, or money order?" I'd get those sentences out as fast as I could, trying to finish my pitch before they could interrupt or hang up. Sitting in a cubicle surrounded by fifteen other telemarketers doing the same thing all day was enough to nearly drive me crazy. Some days, I had to go into the bathroom on an hourly basis, get down on my knees, and just pray to God to get me through the next hour.

During those hard times, there were glimmers of hope. I'd hear great news about someone at a record label really being interested in me and get my hopes up. But it was like fishing. I'd throw my line out, watch the bobber float around, see a fish come over and nibble a bit, but the bobber never goes under and the fish never really takes the hook. I'd be close to having something great happen, then something out of the blue would mess it up. I even had a tornado come through and knock out the power just before I was to do a showcase for a major label. I felt like my life was imitating Murphy's Law, and Murphy had decided to move in next door to me—permanently. There were many times I could have quit. But I didn't, thanks to God and to family. The combination of an incredibly supportive wife and family, faith that God put me here on this earth to make music, and the echo of my dad's advice got me through the dark times and to where I am today. And for that, I will always be thankful.

Zona Jones

Hard-core country music is a way of life in southeast Texas. But Zona Jones didn't grow up with a guitar in his hand. In fact, the son of Texas ranchers preferred riding his horse and hunting over the guitar lessons his parents made him take. But that all changed when Zona saw George Strait in concert. Immediately, he felt a connection to the music he grew up with, remembering the hours he spent with his grandmother listening to his parents' vinyl albums. He fell back in love with country music, picked up the guitar again, and started singing. During law school he sang in nightclubs, and while he was working as a lawyer in Beaumont, Zona and his group became the house band at the famed hot spot Cutters. Balancing a full-time job during the day and playing shows every night, Zona still managed to find time to work on his record in Nashville. Ten years after his Beaumont nightclub debut, *Harleys & Horses* was released, giving Zona a true understanding of the maxim "good things come to those who wait."

Valentine, Texas.
Population 213.

An old switching station for the railroads, Valentine was the closest town to the ranch I grew up on. Every day I made the twenty-five-mile journey into town for school. As you can imagine, making that trip four times a day wasn't feasible for my parents. When I was seven, my dad taught me to drive. Luckily, I was tall for my age, and, with the help of my lunchbox wedged behind me, I could reach the pedals. It was dirt roads almost the whole way; three cattle guards were my biggest obstacle. Otherwise, it was pretty wide open and easy for a seven-year-old to handle. Behind the wheel of an old GMC Jimmy with a big bumper welded onto the front and back, I obeyed my dad's rule of thirty miles per hour. I couldn't get into too much trouble. Once I hit Highway 90, I'd pull off to the side, park the car, and catch the school bus for the last mile of the trip.

Growing up on a 45,000-acre cattle ranch motivated my sisters and me to get an education. My parents made us work very hard. We did daily chores and worked on the weekends (and during the summer). We studied hard and made good grades so we could one day go to college and land a job in an air-conditioned office. As tough as it seemed to us back then, those were probably some of the greatest days of my life.

I spent my afternoons and evenings driving around the ranch with my grandfather, checking on the work crews. If everything was under control, we took off to go hunting as the sun was setting. I loved the time I spent with my grandmother. Growing up as one of twelve children in Depression-era Oklahoma, Granny spent her youth performing live on the radio. Back in those days, music was broadcast over the airwaves by people coming in to the radio station and singing. It was her love of music that inspired me to become a musician. Playing vinyl albums of everyone from Elvis to Engelbert Humperdinck, I'd sing along to the music as she recorded me with a tape recorder. She'd play my songs back, telling me which ones were good and which ones needed more work, so I had quite a music producer at a very young age.

The only real radio station we could get on the ranch was an AM station out of El Paso—X-Rock 80. And on good days, when the weather was just right, our TV antenna on top of the mountain would pick up a station out of EI Paso or Odessa. The only time I really wanted that antenna to work was when the Dallas Cowboys were playing. Roger Staubach was my idol, and I hated missing the Cowboys playing on Sundays. Thankfully, my family members were devout Baptists. Now, this might not seem to have anything to do with Roger Staubach, but it certainly helped make it possible to watch the Cowboys' games. On Sundays, we drove sixty miles to Fort Davis, which had the closest Baptist church. It also had great TV reception. After church, we went to our friends' homes for lunch and the much-anticipated football games. Boy, did I look forward to Sunday school all week long. I guess I have my parents and the Cowboys to thank for introducing me to Jesus Christ, my Savior, and my lifelong devotion to the church. And my family to thank for teaching me the value of hard work and a love of music.

Shannon Lawson

The Kentucky native Shannon Lawson keeps it simple. "There are only two kinds of music, good and bad," he says. A member of the renegade Muzik-Mafia collective, Shannon has devoted his life to making the good kind while often blurring the lines between country, bluegrass, and rock. He spent his childhood cutting and hanging tobacco with his father and four uncles. Wanting to be just like the grown-ups who picked bluegrass tunes on his grandmother's front porch, four-year-old Shannon grabbed his uncle's Epiphone guitar and played until his little fingers were covered in blisters. While Shannon was in college, a seasoned blues musician named Top Hat sauntered into his life and changed everything. Shannon quit school to tour with Top Hat's group, playing the guitar and singing soulful blues covers. Eventually he returned to his roots by forming the Galoots, a bluegrass band that was an electrifying mix of rock and traditional country with a dash of his newly acquired penchant for blues. The prolific singer-songwriter, who never ceases to push the boundaries between music genres, released his debut solo CD, *Chase the Sun*, on MCA in 2002. He has since released an acoustic album, *The Acoustic Livingroom Session*.

I have a family picture from when I was four years old. I'm standing on a hay wagon playing a little plastic guitar and everyone is wearing overalls. We just *look* country. Country is my foundation,

and I had the storybook country upbringing—working on the tobacco farm, playing together as a family on the front porch after
a hard day of working in the fields, and never locking our doors
at night.

The first song I ever played on guitar and sang was "My Heroes Have Always Been Cowboys." I started playing guitar when
I was four, though I didn't get my own guitar till I was seven. We
had a family band, which was unique in my town. When my
cousins and I were four and five years old, we'd be out on the
porch at my grandmother's house playing after dark, after we were
done working in the fields. When I got a little older, I started doing shows at backwoods country places—one was called the Six
Mile Jamboree. These shows brought out deep-woods country
people—some of them weren't even wearing shoes.

I always had a sense of security (founded or not), so I was
never scared about going anywhere. That's how I branched out
from Taylorsville, Kentucky, heading to places I'd never been, or in
some cases never even heard of. There were no worries.

It was the best upbringing for a kid that I can imagine. We
didn't have much money, but we didn't know that at the time. And
I couldn't have asked for a better lesson in the value of hard work.
My grandfather, a sharecropper, taught me how to keep my head
down and stick to my goals. Whether it was pulling the suckers
off the top of tobacco plants as the sun was beating down on me
so I could make enough money to pay for my first year of college
or navigating the highs and lows of the music business, I know
what hard work is. And I'm not afraid of it.

Ty Murray

There was never a question of what Ty Murray was going to be when he grew up. As a toddler, he was riding calves under the Arizona sun and hopping on his mom's sewing machine case in the house. In the fifth grade, his teacher assigned the class an essay answering the question "If you could do anything in your life, what would it be?" Firefighter, astronaut, and doctor were the repeated responses. "I want to beat Larry Mahan's record" was the determined ten-year-old Ty's answer. Rodeo legend Mahan, who won six All-Around World Championships, was Ty's hero and inspiration while growing up. Recognized as the most accomplished rodeo athlete in the century-long history of the sport, Ty fulfilled his fifth-grade declaration by winning a record-setting seven All-Around World Championship titles and earning the well-deserved handle "King of the Cowboys." After achieving his lifelong goals in the sport of rodeo, Ty shifted his focus to riding bulls, winning the 1999 Professional Bull Riders championship and finishing as the reserve PBR Bud Light World Cup Champion for the next three years in a row. In 2000, he was inducted into the ProRodeo Hall of Fame, and in 2004 he took the reins of the PBR, successfully steering the organization to greater mainstream popularity as America's original extreme sport.

D oc. What a great horse. An Appaloosa that pretty much raised my two sisters and me, Doc came into our lives because of some guy who owed my dad money. After skipping town, he called up my dad and said, "Look, Butch, I can't pay you, but why don't you keep that Apple?" So we did. At first, it didn't seem like the greatest trade, since Doc was a young outlaw who wanted to buck. But we worked with him, and he ended up being an amazing horse. Between my two older sisters and me, we won 156 All-Arounds on that horse. That's what you call getting kicked in the ass with a golden horseshoe.

I don't remember the first time I rode a horse, but I also don't remember ever not knowing how to ride a horse. I'm a fourth-generation cowboy, and my family had a two-and-a-half-acre horse-breaking facility. Colts were always on our land, and my mom and I would help my dad out as much as we could.

Waking up at 3:30 in the morning wasn't unusual. In high school I started exercising racehorses at the track. It was a pretty painful endeavor, but I had a driving incentive to do it: I wanted to buy a truck. So I'd roll out of bed, head down to the racetrack, and start riding. In total darkness, I'd ride the first five horses of the morning. I'd usually get about ten to fifteen ridden before I had to take off for school. I'd leave the track, go home, jump in the shower, and head off to school. And it wasn't a bad income for a high school kid—about five bucks a horse. I bought my first truck from riding all those horses. When you have to work that hard to get something, you appreciate it more. You can always tell which kids had their parents buy their cars for them; they were the ones who would tear out of the parking lot spinning their tires.

Ten years ago, I bought my dream. A twenty-two-hundred-acre ranch in Texas. All the riding and the bumps and the bruises were worth it. I had to take all of it to get here. I can look out the big picture window and see wild turkeys pass right in front of me. Deer, bobcats, coyotes, armadillos, squirrels, doves, quail, and pheasants, these are my neighbors out here. I've got privacy, open space, 250 head of mother cows, seventeen horses, three dogs, and a cat.

If it had just been given to me, I don't know that I'd have the same appreciation for it. Working with a colt or passing the afternoon fishing—that's a perfect way to spend a day. At nighttime I feel like I'm in the middle of an enormous black island. It's my version of Disneyland. Being out in the country gives me a sense of peace and calm I can't get anywhere else.

STARS
AND STRIPES

Lee Greenwood

Lee Greenwood's rise to stardom came the old-fashioned way—through hard work and lots of it. Never doubting he was going to be a singer, Lee even missed his own high school graduation so he could play a showroom in Reno, Nevada. Dealing cards at blackjack tables by day and honing his talent in the Nevada lounge "Greenfelt Jungle" by night, Lee finally made the break to Nashville in 1978. A confident, consummate entertainer with nothing to lose, Lee saw his years of patience and persistence pay off in Music City. Two years after his debut album hit the market, he was voted the Country Music Association's Male Vocalist of the Year. The following year he repeated that prestigious feat and added a Grammy for Best Male Country Vocal Performance to his shelf. In 1985, Lee's stirring patriotic song "God Bless the U.S.A." was awarded Song of the Year honors from the CMA. The song gained renewed popularity during the first Gulf War when General Norman Schwarzkopf adopted it as the victorious anthem for America's swift triumph. Following the tragedy of the September 11 attacks, the nation again found comfort in the red, white, and blue anthem, and in 2003 Americans voted it the country's most recognizable patriotic song. A humanitarian through and through, Lee has logged countless miles during his frequent trips to perform for American soldiers stationed across the globe.

My grandparents were sharecroppers, and my grandfather Thomas Jackson was my role model growing up. He taught me about the earth—how to respect the land and understand why things live and why things die. Growing up on a farm outside of Sacramento, I learned to shoot birds to keep them out of the fruit trees, but if I found one wounded, I nursed it back to health. One of the greatest pleasures when I was a kid was following the disc cultivator as it made its way through the fields. All of that turned-up earth brought insects to the surface, and I loved watching the ants and spiders make their way in that tiny world. I realized at a young age that we had a relationship to the earth and that everything was connected.

Every day I milked the cows in the morning and at night. When I was seven, my biggest chore was gathering the eggs from under the hens without getting pecked. It was a challenge. It was in the dark, and if I made a mistake and grabbed the glass egg (the fake egg used to induce the hen to begin laying), I was in trouble. I'd have to go back outside and put it under the hen. If I was really unlucky and it got to be daylight, I'd definitely get pecked when I went back in there.

When I was in high school, one of my chores was to feed a young calf. I used a big bucket with a nipple on it. The calf would lean its chin up over the wooden gate inside the barn, and I would hold the bucket up so it could reach the breakfast of mash. If it started bucking its horns during the feeding, I'd get the bucket dumped all over me, and I'd have to put on another change of clothes before heading off to school.

In a rural area, everything needs your attention at the same time. Farmers work longer than nearly anybody else. They have to get up before the sun and do at least a couple hours of work before they can even think about breakfast. It's the longest job out there. It takes incredible self-reliance and determination to do all of the chores without anyone instructing you. Growing up like that, I knew what my responsibilities were, and I knew they had to be done today. Farms don't wait for tomorrow.

My mother was a piano player, and my father was a woodwind player. My grandparents gave me the privilege of playing music in the house from the time I was very young. I can remember many nights as a kid when I had trouble going to sleep. I was allowed to stay up an extra hour if I played piano in the corner in the dark. We had a little piano set up against the wall, and my grandmother would sit in her chair and listen to me play. Whether I knew what I was playing or not, at least it was some kind of music, and my talent began to emerge. I learned music very much on my own.

We had country radio in the house—even though we were in California, we always listened to Nashville music. We listened to all the Opry stars, and because I was raised during the Beatles era, I became aware of rhythm and blues and rock and roll. Where I was raised there wasn't much entertainment other than in the local bars, so I started playing in them when I was fourteen. In the days of Jimmy Dorsey and Stan Kenton, you'd have a bandstand with the band names plastered on the front of it. We had a dance band called the Moonbeams. There were seven of us, with my sister on the piano, and we'd play a dance for four or five hours and make five bucks. We thought, *All right, yeah, that's good money!* In 1955, when I was a freshman in high school, I played sax in a Dixieland band that opened Disneyland. I was lucky enough to grow up in a family that encouraged these early performing experiences, which helped form the basis for my future in country music.

"God Bless the U.S.A.," a song I wrote in 1983, is strongly tied to patriotism in this country. I think patriotism runs deep in country music due to the geography of the South. The music was honed where the Civil War was fought—a war fought on the grounds of sovereignty and independence. If a Southerner's patriotic nature is challenged or attacked, he or she will have a more militaristic approach to it, more of a defensive reaction than people from anywhere else. Just look at the Alamo. Kentucky, Tennessee, Louisiana, Arkansas, and Texas all came to the rescue. The South is a caring part of the nation—it is the heart of the country. People have a strong feeling of responsibility to take over and protect the home, to think about the greater good, to respond immediately when there is a crisis going on. There is a feeling of "let's go protect this country" and bring the patriotic feeling back to all Americans.

Toby Keith

The award-winning, multiplatinum superstar Toby Keith worked in the Oklahoma oil fields and played defensive end for the Oklahoma City Drillers football team before heading to Nashville in 1993. His debut single, "Should've Been a Cowboy," soared to No. 1 on the *Billboard* country singles chart, and his self-titled debut album was certified platinum. Toby again went platinum with the success of his fifth album, *How Do You Like Me Now?!* With the release of *Unleashed* in 2002, he found himself at the center of public controversy over his song "Courtesy of the Red, White, and Blue," a tribute to his late father's patriotism and faith in the U.S.A. *Unleashed* spent sixty-five weeks on the Top 10 *Billboard* country albums chart and was certified quadruple platinum. A two-time winner of the Academy of Country Music's Entertainer of the Year Award, Toby scored another quadruple-platinum success with 2003's *Shock'N Y'All*. His latest album, *White Trash with Money*, scored platinum status within three months of its release.

I grew up on a little seven-acre farm outside of Oklahoma City. My grandmother ran a supper club, so I grew up around live music and musicians. The first time I went was when I was about three years old. There was a house band that played five times a week—it had a horn section, an upright bass, a baby grand piano, and a guitar. All local musicians. In our house, we were only allowed to listen to my dad's music—Merle Haggard, Bob Wills, a little bit of Willie Nelson every now and then. I was never exposed to other types of music, so I thought my grandmother's house band was just about the hippest thing I'd ever seen. They played everything from "In the Mood" to "Bad, Bad Leroy Brown." Being around that kind of stuff is what got me interested in music. By the time I got my first guitar, when I was eight years old, I knew what I wanted to do with my life.

It breaks my heart to say it, but rock and roll as we know it is gone. But country is still going strong. It's outlasted everything else. It's the kind of music that people can relate to. You don't have to strain to hear the lyrics, and there's always a great message in the music to take away with you. A song has such power—it can give you something to live by, something to make you a better person as you walk through life. Country music reaches out to listeners and gives them something to relate to. It finds a common ground and people are loyal to it.

Country music is the only format that will speak up about patriotism. It is the one format that has enough balls to support this country, and thank God we have it. I've done over sixty shows on the USO tour in support of our troops and our country. No other music format will even touch the topic of patriotism. It's taboo. Country music is also the only one that won't touch anti-American material. It is music that stands up and says, "We are the space between the two sides of the country." The media are so concentrated in Los Angeles and New York City they forget about everything in between, where the real people are. People who listen to their local news instead of the major networks. People who get up every day and put in a hard day's work. People who are worried about the security of this country. People who have sons and daughters, brothers and sisters fighting overseas. Patriotism isn't just supporting the troops. It is having a great love for your country. It's about standing up defiantly when people threaten our country. It is the spirit that says I am an American and I am proud to be an American. And in ten years, when hopefully we will be living in a time of peace, there will still be soldiers stationed around the world protecting us. And I will still be right there with them.

Buck Taylor

The real West is tough country. It's where hardworking men and women worked the land from sunup to sundown and fought to preserve their way of life for generations. Buck Taylor has devoted his life to keeping that memory of the true American West alive. Born the son of the Hollywood actor Dub Taylor, Buck grew up around Western movie greats like John Wayne, Tex Ritter, Big Boy Williams, and Chill Wills, who helped him take his first steps as a baby. After studying art at the University of Southern California, Buck caught the acting bug and starred in numerous top-rated television shows, including an eight-year run on *Gunsmoke*. Since then, he has also starred in films, including 1993's *Tombstone*. In the 1990s, Buck rediscovered his love for art while taking breaks from filming. Describing his west Texas ranch as his "church," Buck uses the American West heritage as a driving inspiration in his artwork. Through his depictions of cowboys, Native Americans, horses, and homesteaders, Buck powerfully conveys the stories of adventure, hardship, and sacrifice that the American frontier was built on.

My memories of being a young man growing up in the San Fernando Valley in California are fantastic. My dad was the actor Dub Taylor, and he was pure country—as were his friends and fans. There were always a lot of hunting dogs around, plenty of doves and quail to eat, and bass fishing. Southern cooking was the regular menu. People were honest and mannerly. Good values were important, and extreme patriotism was a sign of the times. World War II was fought hard with no disrespect between political parties. We were united and proud. I revere my western cowboy heritage and upbringing, and I will not change my lifestyle. If honesty and integrity could rule, this country could get back on track. I loved my upbringing and my folks. And one last thing—God bless the Second Amendment.

Aaron Tippin

As a kid in the mountains of South Carolina, Aaron Tippin fell in love with traditional country sounds while his friends were cranking rock bands on their stereos. Throughout the 1970s, he performed in local honky-tonks, but it took a downturn in the airline industry to spur him to pursue his music with a vengeance. Leaving his career as a commercial pilot behind him, Aaron moved to Nashville and found a welcoming home for his sound during the explosion of new traditionalist country in the early 1990s. His career was launched with his debut single, "You've Got to Stand for Something," a Top 10 song that quickly became a voice of patriotism during Desert Storm. A devoted supporter of American troops, Aaron was the first singer to go to Saudi Arabia during the first Gulf War. In 2002 he went to Afghanistan, and since 2003 he has made annual visits to U.S. forces in Iraq. After enjoying sales of five million albums, Aaron, who cites his late father as his hero and biggest influence, is coming full circle and shaking his sound up with some of the Southern rock roots he grew up with in his latest single, "Ready to Rock (in a Country Kinda Way)."

A hundred-acre farm in the upper west corner of South Carolina is where I spent my childhood—more than enough room for a six-year-old to go out and get lost in. Country kids don't live close together, so you learn to play on your own, to find your independence at an early age. Besides, we had plenty of dogs to keep me company when I was out in the woods: Maco, Gus, Dutch, Blue, Charlie, Harry, Archie, and the best hunter of them all, my dad's German shorthaired pointer named Nell. The second I got off the school bus, I grabbed my shotgun and a dog, and my mom wouldn't expect me home until dark. I can't think of a better way to grow up.

During the week, I had my usual chores of taking care of the cattle, hogs, and chickens. Starting in grammar school, I was a 4-Her, and one year I had a prizewinning market pig that won grand champion at the upper-state fair. If you made it that far, you got into the fair for free, and that was heaven. My dad was a professional pilot, so I only saw him on weekends. When he came home, we were up early, and, boy, we'd hit it. Working the land, planting soybeans, taking care of the crops, cutting hay—I've cut more hay than you can imagine—and we didn't stop until it was dark.

My dad was my role model growing up. My absolute hero. In my world, there is Jesus Christ and, just below him, my dad. When he'd come home on the weekends, I wouldn't leave his side. I was right there with him every chance I could get. I thought he was the greatest thing since sliced bread. He taught me to fly, to hunt, and to fish, and, even though he didn't mean to, he taught me to cuss, too. The way I grew up, and the things I learned from my dad, can be seen in the songs I write. "Workin' Man's Ph.D." and "You've Got to Stand for Something"—they speak to people who are hardworking and fun loving, people who have high admiration for their raising and who love their country.

When I was young, I went to a football game with my dad. The national anthem was playing, and there were a couple of guys a few rows in front of us who were talking through the whole song. When the anthem was over, my dad went right over to them and told them just what he thought about their disrespect. Patriotism means loving your country even when it isn't popular to, being proud without being prodded. Country music speaks to people who love their country. The music and the values of the people who listen to it are interchangeable.

From the time I first went to Nashville, coming off the farm in South Carolina, I knew I had to live in the city for a few years, but I told myself, *Man, I'm headed back out to the country as soon as I can.* The main reason was I wanted my boys to have the kind of childhood I did. I was the luckiest kid on the planet. If I didn't have another day here, my childhood was plenty. That was living. Now I walk through the woods with my boys and I let them lead me around. I want to make sure that even at ages five and eight, they can find their way. "Where's the house?" "Where's the creek?" "How do we get home?" There aren't any signs out in the country, so you've gotta be independent and learn your way. It's a lesson to take you through life. I need my wife and kids and I need to be loved, but I've never been afraid to step out by myself. Learning self-reliance at an early age was one of the best things that growing up in the country gave me.

Scott Whitehead

Never underestimate the value of discipline. Born on a military base and serving as an F/A-18 Hornet pilot during the first Gulf War, Scott Whitehead has always known that behind every success you'll find fierce determination and an unshakable work ethic. A graduate of the prestigious Naval Fighter Weapons School (Top Gun), Scott traded planes for guitars when he moved to Nashville and began working as a staff songwriter with the Acuff-Rose publishing company. Even though he left the Navy, he took his commitment to excellence with him and channeled it into his music career. After he met Ron Kingery, the two decided to form Hometown News, which garnered a Top 40 debut single with "Minivan" and a nomination from the Academy of Country Music for Top Vocal Duo. Even though he spends more time in tour buses than in cockpits these days, Scott still has a strong connection to the armed forces. In 2005, the harmonious vocal duo, who garner comparisons to the Everly Brothers and Simon & Garfunkel with a breezy front-porch flavor, hit the road for a thirty-four-day world tour of military bases.

When the United States was less than seventy-five years old, my great-great-grandfather John Whitehead, along with two brothers, a sister, a wife, and a young son, made an eleven-week trek across the Atlantic from Oldham, England, looking for opportunities in the New World. They took a water route all the way to St. Louis and in 1854 settled in Montgomery County, Missouri. John purchased 120 acres there. My children are the sixth generation to be a part of that land I call home.

The Whiteheads were farmers and coal miners who raised cattle, hogs, corn, and wheat. From below the ground they pulled the black rock more commonly found in the hills of Kentucky than in the rolling plain that is east-central Missouri. The first Whitehead dwelling was a log cabin. A newer homestead was built later from lumber cut on the land. The homestead is now over a hundred years old. It is where my grandfather and father were born, and as long as I have been alive, it has been the gathering place for Thanksgiving and Christmas. My memories are warm and clear of family in the kitchen (the largest room in the house) with the smell of bread and the hint of hickory smoke from a wood-burning stove.

While Dad was growing up, he did his school homework by oil lamp light. When electric lines finally made it to the house, the *Grand Ole Opry* could be heard on Saturday nights all the way from Nashville. Roy Acuff 's "Wabash Cannonball" was a favorite because the actual Wabash Cannonball ran on tracks that passed a few miles away. The famous train's whistle echoed across the land.

My family history and rural life in general have had immeasurable influence on me. Respect for others, respect for the land, and overall love of the U.S.A. are feelings I'm sure I share with millions of other country-based folks. It was love of country and a desire to fly that led me to serve in the military (like my father did) alongside many other like-minded volunteers from all corners of America.

During the first Gulf War I was given orders to fly an F/A-18 across the Atlantic and then on to the aircraft carrier USS *Amer-*

ica stationed in the Red Sea. The jet I flew was a replacement for one that had been lost to enemy fire. During the relatively short eight-hour flight from Jacksonville, Florida, to Rota, Spain, I looked down at the endless water below and could not help but think what a long way we all have come from the arduous journeys our forefathers made on wooden ships to the land of promise.

After eight years of service I made the decision to focus on what has always had the strongest pull in my life—music. So I traded flying F/A-18s for the chance at performing on the country music stage. Seven years of hard work later, Hometown News made its debut on the *Opry*. I know my parents were proud sitting in the audience. It was almost surreal realizing my voice was being broadcast all the way back to the farm on 650 WSM.

THE GREAT OUTDOORS

{ Clint Black }

Growing up in Katy, Texas, as the youngest of four brothers, Clint Black took a fearless step toward a life in music when, at age thirteen, he stole his brother Brian's harmonica. Two years later he taught himself guitar and began to pursue music with an unshakable intensity. After dropping out of high school to play in his brother's band, Clint played the Houston club circuit, soon venturing into songwriting. As the 1990s dawned, so did his music. His first album, *Killin' Time*, launched Clint to international fame with its record-breaking five No. 1 singles and triple-platinum status. By the end of 1990, the vanguard of the "new country" army was headlining his own concert tour and raking in Country Music Association, Academy of Country Music, and American Music Award honors by the armful. That December the country superstar met his future wife, the Houston-bred actress Lisa Hartman, after one of his shows. With his easy grace and unfailing generosity, Clint quickly earned a stellar reputation as a consummate professional in both media and country music circles. In 1993, he and Lisa became the first entertainers to visit U.S. troops stationed in Somalia, and the following year he cut his acting teeth in the television show *Wings* and the movie *Maverick*. An artist who pushes himself in everything he does, Clint again made history by being the first to direct music videos using large-format, 65 mm film. To date, he has charted twenty-eight Top 5 hit singles, sold several million albums worldwide, and performed for a viewership of one billion at Super Bowl XXVIII. In 1996, Clint received a star on the Hollywood Walk of Fame.

oy, I used to do some crazy things as a kid. And I've got the war wounds to prove it. Once, I ripped my knee open in a dirt bike crash. On two different occasions, I fell off my skateboard and got a concussion. Another time, my friend and I were climbing down from our tree house when one of the steps he was on suddenly broke off. He was beneath me, and before he tumbled to the ground, he grabbed my leg and took me with him. I ended up with a broken arm.

But there is one incident in particular that has vividly stuck with me all these years. One day, a few friends and I arrived at a brilliant plan to jump into our bayou right at the source. The source was a dam located at the Addicks Reservoir on the west side of Houston, Texas, where I grew up. When it rained heavily, which was often, the county would open the floodgates, and the raging torrent would rush out, flooding the bayou with rapid-flowing rainwater.

Enter four or five thirteen-year-old boys without life vests, or BRAINS, who jump feetfirst into the rapids for the ride of their lives . . . or deaths, as the case almost was. It wasn't quite dangerous enough to be free-floating in the raging floodwaters careening through the bayou, tearing trees and rocks from the banks. We needed to catch a few venomous snakes along the way. As we drifted along in the current, we would watch out for snakes clinging to debris and try to grab them as we went by. We caught more than our fair share. One snake we thankfully didn't catch was so enormous it nearly made the definition of a "lifetime" only thirteen years for me.

As we came around one bend in the bayou, everyone but me saw the large tree that had been pulled from the banks into the rushing waters in time to get to the banks and to make it around the tree on foot. It lay completely across the bayou, blocking our path. I wasn't able to get to the bank, and the rushing water upon meeting the tree took everything, including yours truly, straight to the bottom. I closed my eyes and began feeling my way through the murky water to a large branch that was heading toward the surface and upstream. It took all my strength to pull myself up the limb to the surface, so when I reached the top, I really needed the breather I expected to get.

The first thing I noticed was the burning in my lungs, sinuses, and eyes. All the things I couldn't wait to use again were on fire. The best I could figure was poison oak. That wasn't the biggest problem! I could've gotten over that with some salve or Benadryl, but the next thing I noticed was all of my friends yelling at me at the top of their lungs. I'm sure I must've thought, *Leave me alone, can't you see I'm trying to drown?* Then I realized they were yelling, "Snake!" Right then I looked straight ahead, right in front of my face, and saw the coiled-up, ready-to-strike water moccasin. That's when I let go of the branch and was sucked right back down to the bottom of the bayou. Now I'd had it.

Miraculously, I found the same limb again and started the arduous climb back to the surface. Somehow I managed to make it again. Have you ever read the instructions on a shampoo bottle? Rinse and repeat. That's what I did. Life-support system on fire, snake in my face, friends yelling frantically, I had no choice but to let go and ride the big suction to the bottom again.

I knew that would be the last time I made that trip because my body was about to give up the ghost. (Fortunately, I still have that ghost, but I try to ignore him when I turn out the lights.) As I was making the last effort to save my own life, one of my friends, Mark Hoag, stepped out to do it for me. He walked out onto the tree, grabbed the snake by the tail, swung it in circles over his head like a lariat, and threw it to the other side of the bayou.

This time, when I returned to the top of my life limb, my friends were screaming the good news. "*Snake's gone! Climb on up!*" I could say we continued our journey down the rapids. But we didn't. My free-floating days were over. But I was thirteen, so it wouldn't be the last stupid choice I would make.

Kix Brooks

A native of swampy Louisiana country, Kix Brooks discovered country music at the source—his neighbor Johnny Horton, one of the most popular honky-tonk singers of the late 1950s. Kix began performing with Horton's daughter as a youth and spent his high school days writing songs and playing in clubs where, he says, "people didn't come to dance so much as to raise hell and have a good time." After working on the Alaskan oil pipeline and hitting the bar circuit throughout the Northeast, Kix moved to Nashville, where he landed a job as a songwriter. His compositions were recorded by Highway 101, John Conlee, and the Nitty Gritty Dirt Band, who scored a No. 1 hit with "Modern Day Romance." After teaming up with Ronnie Dunn, Kix was able to mix his love of songwriting with singing. Debuting in 1991 as a singer-songwriter duo, Brooks & Dunn had success right out of the gate with *Brand New Man*. Their blazing debut reaped five straight No. 1 songs. As one of the most successful collaborations in country music, the multiplatinum-winning force has been honored with four Entertainer of the Year awards and won the Vocal Duo of the Year Award of the Country Music Association a record-setting thirteen times.

My mother was born in Marion, Louisiana, population 608. It's a little town in north Louisiana somewhere between Monroe and Shreveport. It had one of everything—a barbershop, a drugstore, a general store, and a bank. Think of Mayberry and you'll have a pretty good idea of the place.

My grandfather owned the general store and was the loan officer at the bank. I worshipped the ground he walked on, and the time he spent with me left no doubt in my young mind how much I was loved. My mother found a lump in her breast when I was only three years old, at a time when that kind of discovery was pretty much a death sentence. She passed away shortly thereafter, and since my father was a pipeliner and was gone much of the time, I began to spend more and more time in Marion.

I was from Shreveport, the big city, and at first I had a hard time imagining how I would possibly occupy my days in such a place, but grandparents have a way of making everyday things special. I can remember my grandfather taking me out in the backyard, pulling a ripe fig off a tree, biting into it, squinting his eyes, and slowly shaking his head with an appreciation for every nuance of sweetness in the special fruit. He was mad about figs the way a wine connoisseur might connect with the greatness of a fine cabernet. It was nothing for us to drive forty miles to Ruston for a box of peaches—a peach wasn't just something in a grocery store, it was something to be appreciated. God had made a special piece of ground to grow them for "all they were worth," and we would make the trek and talk about how good they had tasted for weeks to come. And Friday night, if all had gone well during the week, was a night for celebration. We would drive twenty-five miles to Farmerville to the A&W for a hamburger and a root beer that came in a frosted mug—if you didn't like that, you didn't like living.

I began joining my grandfather in the daily care of not only the tomatoes in his garden but also the three rows of roses he constantly pruned, dusted, and watered. I learned the importance of not only something good to eat but also the beauty of what God gives us for the centerpiece on a dinner table.

My favorite part of the week, and I believe his, too, was Tuesdays and Thursdays—those were the days he worked at the bank, and as far as I can tell, he spent the better part of his meetings interrogating his customers on where the fish were biting. I would be sitting on the front porch when he would turn the corner down the street coming home, and I could tell by the grin on his face whether or not he had the goods! It was not just the location we were looking for, but also the bait and equipment. It might be fly rod or rod and reel, minnows, or purple worms, but he would find out, and we would acquire whatever it took to make the catch.

Well, the day I'm thinking of now was a hot one in July, and the news about the fishing was from old Homer Wilson, who was a very reliable source. It seems after several really bad storms, the Ouachita River had come out of its banks, and the woods in one particular area my grandfather happened to be familiar with were flooded. Somehow, Homer had figured out that the "bream," as we called 'em (known as perch to a lot of people), were biting like crazy—seems what they were really crazy about, though, was something called a catalpa worm. I could tell my grandfather was very excited at this opportunity. Bream aren't the biggest fish in the world—nothing like the largemouth bass we often fished for, or the big catfish we would sometimes hook on our trotlines in the river—but when they were biting, there was nothing quite so fun as seeing the cork going down and the cane pole bending double, not to mention the thrill of what might be on the other end of the line.

First we went to a neighbor's house whose yard had a catalpa tree, and my grandfather pointed out the caterpillars inching their way across the low-hanging limbs. We smiled at each other and

began plucking them off and dropping them in a bucket we nor-
mally used to keep crickets in. The worms were about three
inches long and what I called juicy. After we had a couple of
buckets full, we loaded up our old tin boat, known in those parts
as a johnboat (I have no idea why), and our little outboard motor
and took off down a dusty red dirt road in my grandfather's 1951
Chevy pickup. The windshield was broken with two big bull's-eye
spiderwebs where rocks had tried to bounce through on previous
trips.

We arrived at a place where the floodwaters started. We eased
our boat in the water, pushed away, and headed into the flooded
woods until we finally came to a place that looked good to us.
This was the moment of truth. My grandfather carefully untan-
gled our poles, and then reached down into the bucket, picking
just the right creepy crawler, and I watched carefully as he ran a
hook back and forth through the caterpillar. He looked at me as
if to say, "You got it?" I followed suit, and we dropped them in
the water. The corks stood up straight when the worms were all
the way down, and then they both went under. *Oh yeah*, this was
what we'd come for. With some effort, we both pulled up a fish,
and, as far as bream went, these babies were big—"full-hand-
sized," we called 'em. We dropped them in the cooler and loaded
up again—*oh yeah, two more, wow!* Now, this wasn't fishing—this
was catching.

We were both laughing and whooping it up when my grandfather said, "All right, let me show you something." About three
feet up from his hook he took the line and made a special knot
that wouldn't slip and tied on another line with another hook on
it—he did the same for me—and now we each had two hooks going down at the same depth on our poles. Could this really work?
I loaded up my two worms and dropped them in the water. The
cork went down, and I started to pull up when he said, "Hang on

a second." Then I felt another tug. "Now pull it up, Kix," he said. *Woooohooooo!* Two fish on the same pole! We caught fish until they finally slowed down, and then we moved and did it again. We filled a metal Coleman cooler to the top, and threw out the small ones that were alive, until it was full of the biggest, prettiest perch I had ever seen. What a day.

The sunset was painting the flooded timber in reds and yellows that you have to go to Louisiana and creep through a swamp to truly appreciate. And then came the words I dreaded most: "Okay, pal, it's getting late, we better head back." I knew we had gone deep into the timber and we would be lucky to make it back before dark as it was, so I packed up my pole, and my grandfather pulled the cord and fired up the old johnboat and pointed us back through the trees. We were making good time, and both of us kept opening the icebox, looking at the packed cooler, and giving the thumbs-up as we cut a trail through the water and the trees.

Nothing quite so soothing as the steady hum of an outboard when all of a sudden—*Bam! Whack! Whacky whack!* And then quiet. My eyes were wide. I knew we had hit something—probably a stump—it had happened many times before. As my grandfather pulled the engine out of the water, I waited nervously for the "okay," but all he did was stare. I could tell he wasn't so much looking at the back of the engine as wondering what we would do next. I carefully moved to the back of the boat so as not to tip us and got a look for myself. Generally, the worst that would happen would be a bent propeller. I knew they were expensive, so maybe that was it. But what I saw was the shiny metal shaft dripping water where the propeller used to be and the dark water underneath. "I can swim down and try to find it D-Daddy" (the name us kids called him). I had certainly dived for pennies in the pool at the Y enough and was no stranger to swimming in muck like this, as that was all we had around Marion. I just wanted to get that look

off his face. "We've already drifted a ways," he said. "Do you remember how deep we were fishing? It must be eight to ten feet
deep here, and we don't have a cotter pin to hold it on, if you were
to get lucky," he said as he looked up at the sky. "Grab a paddle,
we've got a trip ahead of us." I felt important that I was included
in the task at hand, but it was starting to get dark now, and I knew
before long it would be "sure 'nuf" dark.

This was a time before cell phones and trolling motors, and
lots of other things that have made life too easy or too compli-
cated, depending on how you look at it. For a while we paddled in
silence, discouraged by our bad luck, and then my grandfather
said, "You know what? We've got a *real* problem here." I thought
to myself, *Oh no! Now what?* After weighing all the negatives we
were facing and wondering what I might have missed, I said,
"Sir?" I couldn't really see it, but I could hear the smile in his voice.
"Well," he said, "we've got all these good fish here on ice, your
grandmother has gotten the grease hot by now, and pretty soon
Lawrence Welk will be coming on. She won't be worried about us
near as much as missing the Lennon Sisters, so when she goes
running in to watch 'em, that grease is liable to get too hot and
catch on fire, it'll start in the kitchen, and by the time we get
home, she'll be standing in the front yard crying, watching the
house burn down, and it'll be all our fault. And the worst of it is
we won't be able to fry these fish!" We both started laughing and
I felt better.

I was paddling with a longer paddle to keep us moving, and he
was using a short one on the front, pulling and steering us along
with one strong arm. We didn't have much of a moon, but it was
enough once our eyes adjusted. To this day I'm still amazed at the
confidence he showed easing us through the darkness—courage is
contagious, and the conversation continued as we quietly passed
one tree after the other. I can still see them in my mind like giant

cutout silhouettes in the flooded woods. We talked about our previous fishing trips, my cousins, our dogs, music, my mother dying, Jesus, and finally he told me the story of the night his son was born. I had no idea he ever had a son. I must have been eight or nine, and no one had ever mentioned this to me. He told me how the baby was not doing well when it was born, and the doctors didn't know what they were doing, and he drove it down to Baton Rouge, some three hundred miles away, but they couldn't save him. Wow, I never knew. Years later, I asked my aunt Grace about it, and she told me how the baby had been stillborn. My grandfather had gone half-crazy and took the lifeless infant in his car, in a horrible pouring-down rainstorm, all the way to Baton Rouge thinking it was still alive. It made me sad to hear that the man I idolized, someone so strong, could ever have been so out of control, but it also made me realize the power of a broken heart. I know now just how much those days we spent together must have meant to him, most likely as much as they meant to me. When I was growing up, people always said I was the son he never had, but honestly I think I was just his grandson and that was plenty.

Our talk went back to lighter topics like the new coach of the Little League team and how to arrange your cards while playing gin. I was just about to think maybe we were actually lost, when we made an abrupt stop and heard the welcome sound of the bottom of our boat on river sand. We both let out a big *"Woooooooooo!!!"* He knew where we were the whole time! Turns out this was timber where he had invested money, which meant he had also invested time—he said, "You never got one without the other." He shined a flashlight over at our old truck. "You had a flashlight?" I asked. "Why didn't you use it?" "Because I didn't need it," he answered. "What if we had trouble with the truck or something else? I was saving our batteries." That's the way he operated. We loaded up the boat and tied it down, taking one last look in that cooler at all those fish, and life was good again. I jumped in the truck beside him, and he said, "Why don't you sing me something, little man?" I sang everything I knew at the top of my lungs.

Years later, I went to visit him while I was going to music school at Louisiana Tech. He took me for a ride down an old logging road to see some property he'd bought. He'd always wanted me to be a doctor, but that day he spoke to me seriously about my potential in music, and hearing that from him made my ambitions seem legitimate. I always wanted to make him proud, and I couldn't help thinking back to his wanting me to sing that night. I don't remember falling asleep after the lost-propeller adventure, but I do remember waking up when we got home, and of course my grandmother hadn't been watching TV. She was worried sick—standing by the front gate. The grease was still hot, though, and after we took our scolding, we had fried fish, hush puppies, and fresh onions and tomatoes out of the garden. It's hard to describe just how good it tasted that night, but I'll bet anyone who's ever loved his granddaddy can imagine.

{ Helen Cornelius }

"If you believe in yourself, then nothing is gonna knock you down," says Helen Cornelius, a Missouri native who grew up playing music with her seven brothers and sisters on their family's farm. As far back as she can remember, Helen had a yearning for adventure and a vision of her destiny. At age five, she made her singing debut in a talent show, which she would continue to perform in for years. However, it was her abilities as a songwriter that burst her onto the Nashville music scene. During the late 1970s, her songs were recorded by some of country's biggest artists, including Reba McEntire and the Oak Ridge Boys. After RCA Records executives heard the gifted songwriter's voice, Helen scored her first major recording contract. The serendipitous teaming up with Jim Ed Brown produced several hit singles like "I Don't Want to Have to Marry You" and "I'll Never Be Free," as well as the coveted Country Music Association's award for Vocal Duo of the Year. During the 1980s, Helen focused on her solo career and indulged her flair for Wild West sharpshooting in a touring production of *Annie Get Your Gun*. In the 1990s, she opened a Tennessee dinner theater, where she performed nightly for five years. Helen continues to grace the stage of the Grand Ole Opry and keeps up a busy tour schedule, performing both in solo concerts and with Jim Ed Brown. No matter how busy her life gets or how many awards are bestowed on her, Helen never forgets the little Missouri farm girl with big dreams. "I feel so blessed to be able to make a living doing something I love so much," she says with a gracious smile.

hores and more chores—that's the fate of children growing up on a farm. Daddy had tilled the garden; the rows were hollowed out and ready for that season's offering—and ready for our young, agile frames to bend and plant.

Sister Judy and I were given planting instructions along with a quart jar of dried sweet peas. We made the long trek to the top of the hill to that year's garden plot and began the tedious process of planting. We knew the instructions by heart: just so deep, just so far apart, then lightly cover with soil.

Boring! Judy devised the plan to dig a hole, dump the quart jar of peas in the hole, cover them up, and tell Daddy we were through. (I can blame it entirely on her as this is my story.)

Once the burial was completed, we covered the prepared rows over so they at least appeared to have been planted and headed home, our story intact. However, we returned much too soon. Momma knew we could not possibly have finished that task in so short a time. She told Daddy. Oh, boy. That's when we marched right back to the garden plot with Daddy while he took a break from plowing another field. No surprise—his investigation revealed no peas in the covered rows, but nearby, a freshly dug grave, complete with a mound, and, of course, all of the peas. After an encounter with a peach tree switch and a lot of tears, we returned to the site and planted the peas . . . one pea at a time.

Brad Cotter

Learning to sing as soon as he could walk, the rebellious son of a Baptist preacher became a household name after winning the USA Network's *Nashville Star* competition in 2004. Raised on gospel music in Opelika, Alabama, Brad Cotter recorded five gospel albums during his childhood and teens but delved into playing country, rock, and blues at juke joints and frat houses all over the Southeast. After Brad paid his dues in Nashville for more than ten years, along came the reality show that proved to be his long-awaited big break. Brad thought it was worth a shot—even if he made it on one week of the show, other doors might open for him. Fast-forward nine weeks and Brad was voted by millions of viewers as the next Nashville Star. Doors started to open everywhere. His debut album, *Patient Man*, was released in July 2004, and its hit single, "I Meant To," broke the record for the highest chart debut by a new country artist since 1990.

I have a picture in my mind of standing beside my mother in the doorway of the mobile home my adolescent parents and I lived in at the time as we were looking out and watching my grandfather drive slowly up the winding gravel road that stretched in front of the old home place and led down to the barn. He was loaded down with beef cattle and heading out to the auction in Montgomery, Alabama. Obviously, since I was barely two years old at the time, I was unaware of any of this. But I can remember the bright yellow lights across the cab of the big truck. I can't recall her exact words, but I remember my mother pointing out the fact that my daddy and granddaddy were in that truck.

I have hundreds of fond memories that I love to recall about growing up in the country. I don't have to think very hard to remember how fortunate I was to have grown up in such circumstances. I know, I know, we lived in a trailer! And better than that, it was practically in my grandparents' front yard. Sounds far from fortunate to some, but what some folks don't understand is that it was never about the place we lived in. It was always about the land, the community, making the best of what we had, and, most important to me, having access to all the wonderful things a little boy can learn about God's wonderful creation, where you can have room to roam and explore all the awesome things nature has to offer. That's where the fine people in the community come in as well. As we all know, oftentimes little boys need some boundaries, and I was certainly no exception to this. I was definitely a community effort. I'm convinced that my parents could have hired an entire team of babysitters to watch over me and I still would've found some sort of mischief. There was no more perfect place for all of my adventures to play out than on that little farm in Ridge Grove, Alabama.

You see, I had the best of both worlds as a kid. When I was three, my dad took a job with the Uniroyal tire company, so my parents and I moved to the city of Opelika. Although this is a far cry from what you might consider urban, when compared with the country, we had indeed moved to town. I was fortunate to have friends and neighbors close by and have access to all the conveniences of town. But in just thirty minutes I could be on my horse named Bo (after the former Auburn running back Bo Jackson) and roaming the rolling hills of some of the most beautiful scenery you can imagine, without seeing or hearing another two-legged creature. Boy, did I love it! I would pretend to be Billy the Kid out on the frontier. Granddaddy, Uncle Harold, and Dad were in my outlaw gang. Of course, to the men who were rounding up the cattle, mending the fences, caring for the critters, and so on, these little adventures were known as "work." Fortunately, I was usually encouraged to mostly stay out of the way when the real work was taking place. But, hey, more time to explore nature and quench my insatiable thirst for mischief, right? I wish I could say I was relieved of all chores, but as anyone who's ever spent much time around a farm will tell you, there's always plenty of work to be done, so everybody has to chip in. I wouldn't take anything for the memories attached to some of those hardworking days I got to share with my grandfather.

One particular memory that stands out for me was also one of my most valuable learning experiences concerning nature and respecting animals. It was a typical mid-July morning in southeast Alabama . . . hot. It's just after sunrise, and the dew is still on the ground, along with a hazy mist standing just inches above the grass that makes the pastures almost look like swampland. It was extremely humid, and I'm sure it was almost nine hundred degrees in the shade already. Granddaddy (a.k.a. Doc Holliday) and I (The Kid) had just topped a ridge about three hundred yards behind the barn, when out across the foggy pasture ran a doe and her baby fawn. Well, being that I was about twelve years old at the time, I thought I would sound like a real man to my fellow podna in crime when I blurted out: "Boy, I sure wish I had my shotgun right now. I'd kill 'em both with one shot!" My grandfather then begins to tell me in his slow, methodical way how that scenario could have played out. "You see," he said, pausing, "if you hit the fawn, then the mother will have lost her young. But if you hit the mother, then the fawn will have no mother and eventually die, too.

So it sounds to me like you would have no choice but to hit them both with one shot now, would you?" I waited, because I knew there was more. "Now then, that's not to mention the fact that your grandmother just fed us a feast for breakfast"—I couldn't argue with that, since she did this three times a day no matter what—"and you know we have plenty to eat. They aren't causing any harm, so killing them for no reason wouldn't be right, now, would it?" We both knew he was right.

Don't get me wrong. I *love* to hunt and fish! I grew up doing so. But I've also grown up with a respect for nature that I believe is taught by people like my granddaddy. Thanks to him, I know the difference between just killing something for the sake of shooting it, to say you shot it, and hunting and fishing with respect for Mother Nature and the laws and regulations we have in place to protect her. I enjoy nature's bounty; I just don't abuse it. And besides, I'm too darn lazy to clean fish, so I always practice catch and release anyway. I would've never made it on the wild frontier.

I loved growing up on the farm, swimming and fishing in the rivers and streams, summers on the backwater at my grandmother's lake house, all the fine gospel singings, Friday night fish fries, SEC football, mud-ridin' in our 4x4s (which was mostly just a way to try to impress the pretty little southern belles without having to think of something cool to say), the sounds of crickets and tree frogs singing you to sleep at night, and homemade ice cream. Not only do I feel extremely blessed to have been born in this great country we live in, but I am so very grateful to God for letting me grow up country.

Joni Harms

There was a time when country music was called country-and-western. It was a time when Marty Robbins, Gene Autry, and Tex Ritter ruled the airwaves. Somewhere down the music road, the "western" was dropped. But Joni Harms never forgot about it. Singing about family and home, enduring love, hard work, and good, clean fun, Joni stays true to the western roots that were instilled in her while growing up on the Oregon ranch that her great-great-grandfather settled in the 1870s. While she has toured around the world, makes frequent trips to Nashville, and performs at national venues like the Grand Ole Opry and Carnegie Hall, Joni has planted her own roots at her ancestral home and keeps it running as a horse and Christmas tree ranch. Named the Female Vocalist of the Year by the Western Music Association in 2003, Harms is also an acclaimed rodeo queen. With an emphasis on bringing back traditional western values, Joni's music shines with visions of cowboys, horses, wide-open land, and hearty ranch living. Her latest album, *That's Faith*, is composed of songs with a Christian message.

I'm proud to say our ranch has been in the Harms family for over a hundred years. I have a very strong connection to this place and, in my songs, I often write about it. With all the traveling I have done with my music, it is wonderful to be able to come back to a place where once I pull in the driveway I know *I'm home*.

My favorite time of year was calving season. It was my job to check on the cows each morning before getting ready for school. One morning my horse, Midnight, and I found a special surprise. In a tall patch of green grass, Midnight stopped in his tracks and let out a snort. Special surprise, indeed! Not one but twin Black Angus calves! We raced back to give Dad the report, and it was such big news it even made our local paper.

I love being from the country, and I love bringing up Olivia and Luke (my children) in the same place I was raised. I think there is a certain something about folks from the country. I think you learn how to make the best of what you have, and that may not always be a lot. I also think you learn to "cowboy up" and pick yourself up when you get bucked off.

This way of life has been around for ages, forming the heroes of our childhood—Roy Rogers, Dale Evans—people who were the good guys. It's always great to see the good guys win, and even better when they're good ol' cowboys.

Justin McBride

Whoever says the third time's the charm never met Justin McBride. At just four years old, the Nebraska native dreamed of being a world-champion bull rider. Once he entered the sport's elite group of riders, lack of experience, bad luck, and major injuries, including a punctured lung and broken ribs, kept the fearless competitor from realizing his life's ultimate goal for three years in a row. But in 2005, the fourth time proved to be his lucky charm. The entire season came down to the last few rides in Las Vegas. After what many consider to be the most nail-biting, heart-pounding, miraculous seventy-five-point ride in history, twenty-six-year-old Justin hung on to a formidable bull named Camo and won his long-awaited world championship. With the presentation of the legendary gold buckle, Justin's name went down in the history books, and his childhood fantasy was fulfilled.

Growing up with thousands of acres to roam on is heaven. Hunting and fishing, getting as dirty as I wanted, I got to be a real kid. Living on a working ranch meant spending all day with my family. My dad didn't leave in the morning for an office. The ranch was his office. I got to trail around with him, setting to work on any chore he gave me. Every night we sat down to a family dinner, and during the summers we ate three meals a day together. My mom's special dinner of breaded steak fingers with mashed potatoes and gravy is still my favorite. If I wasn't asleep, I was riding a horse, branding cattle, riding bulls, or camping with my buddies. With our sleeping bags, some snuff, and a few beers we managed to sneak into our bags, we'd head down to the river and build a lean-to with old limbs we cut off the trees. With our BB guns, we'd run around pretending to be hunting. When I got a little older, I'd take my 1967 Ford truck—a pretty sweet ride— for a drive down the main drag in town. Some nights, if we had a good snow under a full moon, my friends would come over to hunt coyotes.

I wouldn't change a thing about the way I grew up. I loved everything about it. Going to rodeos in the summer and calving out the cows during the winter—it was hard work, but I loved it. That's the thing about ranching. You've got to really like what you're doing because sometimes it's working daylight to dark and the pay's not that great. But having a connection to the land is worth every second of hard work. Now I've got my own ranch and my own daughter. I want her to grow up with the same kind of connection. I want to teach her to take care of the grass, the wildlife, and the livestock, to respect the land, and to leave it better than when she got it. That's what loving the country means.

Craig Morgan

A walk outside with the cheeping of crickets filling your ears. Jumping on a three-wheeler and tackling the woods, unable to wipe the smile from your face for the whole ride. Heading out in a fishing boat as the sun gently rises. The small moments that are often brushed over because of life's hectic pace are what Craig Morgan celebrates in his music. During his eleven years in the military, this native Tennessean developed a deep appreciation for the tiny moments of perfection that he used to take for granted. While stationed in Panama, he was averaging two hours of sleep a night and dealing with a deluge of gunshots during the day. He was in survival mode and didn't have time to think about home. But when he got to Korea, Craig could finally catch his breath. And he had time to think. Memories from home came flooding into his head and onto the page. As soon as he returned stateside, Craig recorded demos and worked any job he could find to pay the bills. In 2000 he released his first album, and in 2003 his second album, *I Love It*, produced his first hit single, "Almost Home." He has hit the road with such country music giants as Montgomery Gentry, LeAnn Rimes, and Brad Paisley. His most recent release is 2005's *My Kind of Livin'*.

Every afternoon, the second the school bus dropped us off, my next-door neighbor and I would take our shoes and socks off, roll our pants up, rip our shirts off, and walk the creek up to our houses, using our shirts to catch fish. The fish were these little old bottom-feeders called hog suckers. Once they were in shallow water, it wasn't too hard to catch them. Then I'd head home for schoolwork and our family dinner. The smell of meat loaf and mashed potatoes and homemade biscuits made my mouth water as soon as I got home. Once we sat down at the table, nobody dared to take a bite until everyone was served. Those minutes seemed to last forever. First my mom served my dad. Then the four kids' plates were served, and finally she'd sit down to her plate of food. But we still had a blessing to get through. If we reached for anything before the blessing was finished, we got a swift spoon to our knuckles or a quick thump on our hands.

Music was always a huge part of our lives. Every weekend, my dad was out playing bass at shows. He regularly played on *The Ralph Emery Show* and at a place in middle Tennessee called the Jingo Jamboree. All the kids would hang out while the band played, running around backstage and trying not to get into trouble. Every now and then my dad would bring me up onstage and force me to sing. I honestly don't remember if I liked it or disliked it. What I do remember liking was the fact that when I was done my dad would give me a quarter.

I started writing songs long before I joined the military. But I think leaving home and leaving the country to experience other cultures put me in a place and environment where the only way that I could truly express what I was feeling was through songwriting. After eleven years of active duty, I missed home. I missed my family. And I really missed the outdoors. No matter where I went in the world, there was no outdoors like the outdoors at home. The smell, the trees, the creeks, the water, the grass—just everything was better back home. When I finally made it back, I was surprised at how small everything was. That creek I caught hog suckers in seemed so small, and the three-rope bridge that I always used to cross that creek was tiny. It always seemed like such a long way to get across when I was young, but suddenly I could jump from one side of the creek to the other.

I'm still country. I have my own family, and we live on a dirt road. My kids know the difference between an oak tree and a hickory tree. They know where to find ginseng. They know what mushrooms you can eat and what you can't eat. They know how to hunt. They know how to survive in the woods. They know how to respect their elders, and they know the importance of the words "Yes, please, ma'am" and "No, thank you, ma'am." Out here, I can appreciate the little things in life. And they're usually right in front of you: cool grass under your feet, a blowing wind that makes the limbs of a tree sway, crawdads that swim off backward after you turn over the rocks in a creek—the things that people overlook are the things that are the most powerful.

{ J o s h   T u r n e r }

Sometimes destiny deals you a hand of cards that you just have to play. It happened to Josh Turner one night as he was walking across the campus of Belmont University. Without enough money to buy the recently released complete Hank Williams box set, Josh went to his alma mater's library to check it out. Sitting in a little cube with the headphones pushed tightly to his ears, he listened for hours to the rare demos of Hank and his guitar. When he left the library, Josh noticed how intensely dark the night was. Suddenly he had a vision of wide-open plains with a track running down the middle. Out of the darkness, a long, sleek, shiny black train came roaring down the tracks. People were standing all around not knowing what to do—should they get on or just stay put? When he got home that night, Josh grabbed his guitar, sat on his bed, and let the haunting song about temptation and redemption pour out of him. "Long Black Train" was presented to the public during Josh's debut on the *Grand Ole Opry* in 2003. When he was called for an encore, the stunned singer, whose smooth baritone leaves crowds speechless, managed to get halfway through the first verse before getting choked up. He knew his life was about to change dramatically. One month later, he signed with MCA Nashville and released his debut album, *Long Black Train*. By the following year, it had been certified platinum. In 2006, his album *Your Man* defied the sophomore slump and resulted in a No. 1 single on *Billboard*'s country airplay chart and a No. 1 slot on the country album chart.

Paradise is where I grew up. At least that's what I call it. The real name is Hannah, South Carolina, and it was out in the country, among the farms and fields, the pine trees, and the dirt roads. The second I was finished with my chores, I was off to the river to fish. My daddy and I fished on the Lynches River, right behind our house. A small black water river surrounded by wetlands, it's the most beautiful river I've ever seen. My favorite memories are of early mornings on that pristine river, drifting downstream together in my grandaddy's johnboat, with no worries, nowhere we had to be. It was a time for us to get away and just be surrounded by the things God created and the beauty that he's given us. We became more than father and son on those trips—we became friends.

My daddy wasn't afraid to tell it like it was. "Josh," he said, "sometimes you have to do things that you just don't want to do." A simple statement, but it was something I needed to hear. As a hardheaded and stubborn kid, I knew there were plenty of things I needed to do but I just didn't want to. School, relationships, everyday situations—it was starting to cause problems for me. With that simple advice, Daddy made me realize that I had to be brave, courageous, and wise in my decision making. The right decision isn't always the one that's the easiest.

Performing at the April Fools for Christ church benefit was something I absolutely did *not* want to do. My mama had put up twenty-five dollars each for my brother, my sister, and me to get onstage and perform. To get out of it, you had to pay the same amount. Well, none of us had anywhere close to twenty-five dollars, so we were all stuck. My brother impersonated the supreme nerd Steve Urkel, my sister tap-danced her way across the stage, and I got trapped into doing Randy Travis's "Diggin' Up Bones." I was scared out of my mind. Other than singing songs in the

Union Baptist Church ("Arky, Arky" was the song I made my church singing debut with at the age of four!), I'd never sung in front of a crowd before. I got up there with my knees practically shaking, and I remembered what my dad told me. So I did it. And it was one of the best things I could have done. It was the first moment I realized I knew what I wanted to do with my life.

I just love where I come from. It truly is heaven to me. People drink sweet tea and eat real home cooking. Neighbors wave at you as they drive by, and long evenings are spent on the front-porch swing. It's an honest way to live, and no matter how long I've been gone or how far I've traveled, when I'm heading back to Hannah, there's a certain point on the highway where my body just relaxes. My mind clears. I start smiling. And I know I'm home.

Carrie Underwood

Dreams really do come true. Just ask Carrie Underwood. The daughter of a paper mill worker and an elementary school teacher, Carrie fell in love with singing as a little girl in the church choir. By the time she reached college, her attention was devoted to academic studies. During summers, she performed in country shows at her college, but Carrie thought a career in the music business was a long shot. Little did she know what fate had in store for her. During her senior year in college, auditions were being held for the hit reality television show *American Idol*. Encouraged by her friends and family, she decided to go for it. Carrie and her mom jumped in the car and drove all night to get to the open audition in St. Louis. After a few callbacks, she received the news that she was heading to Hollywood on her first-ever plane ride. Stunning the judges and millions of viewers with her powerful voice and girl-next-door charm, Carrie burst to international stardom as 2005's *American Idol* winner. "Inside Your Heaven," her first single, soared up the charts, making Carrie the first country music artist to debut at No. 1 on *Billboard*'s Hot 100. Her album, *Some Hearts*, quickly went triple platinum and solidified this talented artist as one of music's hottest young stars. In between collecting Country Music Television and Academy of Country Music awards, watching her debut country singles reach the top of the charts, and performing for her fans across the United States, Carrie graduated magna cum laude from Northeastern State University in 2006.

The most wonderful memories that I hold in my heart come from the place where I grew up. I was fortunate enough to be born in Oklahoma—outside a small town called Checotah. There are many reasons I cherish my childhood and the place that I spent it. One is that I got to spend much of it outdoors.

I will never forget playing with my best friend, Marcy, who lived down the street. Her grandfather lived next door to me, and she and I would play in his yard. We would spend countless hours climbing trees and swinging from their branches as her grandpa peeled apples for us. Her grandfather also had a cherry tree and a garden, which we would help him harvest. In turn, he would let me take tomatoes home to my parents. My mother would leave the porch light on for me, and if it got too dark, she would walk out on the porch and call my name so I would know it was time to go in for the night.

For me, the country also held many of nature's wonders. I know my mother probably got sick and tired of all the little creatures I would bring home to play with. I can't even begin to count the number of tadpoles, frogs, turtles, snakes, rabbits, and other animals I would catch, play with for a day or so, and return to the wild. I remember one time a wild baby rabbit got loose in the house (my fault) and stayed on the loose for about a week! We finally caught it and let it go. I got in trouble, but it was a really fun week! Needless to say, rabbits were no longer welcome in the house!

Another great memory of growing up in the country is how much time I got to spend on or near the water. We lived about an hour from the lake, so fishing and boating were quite common. Summer, sunshine, and water go hand in hand.

One of the most wonderful things about being outside a lot as I grew up was how much fun I could make for myself. Instead of playing video games or watching television, I loved to do simple things like play with my dog or play in the pasture as my parents worked with the cows. I would fill up jugs of water and take them down to my parents, who were working in the hot sun, and "help" them. I use that term loosely because I am sure I was only in the way, but my parents seemed to welcome the cold water anyway!

Sometimes when I tell people who are from "the city" where I am from, I know they look at me with a little pity. Most likely they think that there is much I have never experienced. They may think I am simple and have missed out on city life. But in fact, it is I who pity them. They are the ones who have missed out on the best parts of life. I would never trade my childhood for anything in this world. Someday, I want my children to grow up in Oklahoma just like I did because the best people in the world come from the country!

MUSIC

Bill Anderson

"If you want someone's attention, whisper." Old advice that proves to be true for the country legend Bill Anderson. With his breathy voice and warm, soft singing, "Whisperin' Bill" has been writing, performing, and recording country music for over forty years. Trying his hand at songwriting when he was nineteen years old, Bill composed the country classic "City Lights" and began to stake his claim in music history. His exceptional talent for both writing and performing has set him apart in the industry as a first-rate musician who can write hits for others as well as produce his own chart-topping singles. Bill has been a member of the Grand Ole Opry since 1961, and his richly deserved place in the upper echelons of music history was cemented with his induction into the prestigious Country Music Hall of Fame in 2001. Some might have slowed down after that honor. Not Bill. In 2005, he and Jon Randall took home the Country Music Association's Song of the Year Award for the poignant ballad "Whiskey Lullaby," recorded by Brad Paisley and Alison Krauss. Never one to rest on his music laurels, Bill has also taken on the field of television as the first country artist to host a network game show. He also appeared for three years on ABC's *One Life to Live*. Not knowing the meaning of "taking a day off," Bill released the album *The Way I Feel* in 2005, and he is actively involved in radio's newest incarnation as the host of a show on XM Satellite Radio.

I grew up country in the city.

That might sound like a contradiction, but it's not.

I was born in Columbia, South Carolina, at the time a town of some sixty thousand friends 'n' neighbors. My family later moved to the outskirts of Atlanta, Georgia, again not exactly what you'd call rural America.

But I grew up country. I spent a lot of time with my grand-papa Anderson, who was an old-time fiddle player. My grand-mama Anderson picked guitar, and my granddaddy Smith was a genuine circuit-riding preacher. There was an Anderson Family Band, a six-hundred-acre Anderson homestead full of more aunts, uncles, and cousins than you could shake a stick at, and, across the road from the farm, an Anderson family cemetery with head-stones that dated back to the nineteenth century.

My grandmama could whip up the best mess of homegrown collard greens a young boy ever sank his teeth into. She'd urge me to eat all I could hold, and then I'd watch as she'd pour the left-over juice across the top of a hot slab of her homemade corn bread. My grandpapa called it "pot likker," and I thought that was the funniest word I had ever heard.

The first music I ever heard on the radio was by Byron Parker and his Hillbillies on the radio station WIS in Columbia. I cut my teeth listening to Snuffy Jenkins roll his fingers and thumb across a five-string banjo, not knowing that a man named Earl Scruggs was listening and learning from that same Snuffy Jenkins some two hundred miles up the road in the hills of North Car-olina. I listened to deep-voiced Texas Jim Robertson sing "Rain-bow at Midnight" from a network studio in New York, and I can still remember the sponsors, folks like Good Enough flour, Black Draught laxative, and Seiberling tires. I thought Byron

Parker's song "How Many Biscuits Can You Eat?" was the national anthem.

I learned early in life that country is not a place on a map. Country is a place in your heart. In your soul. In the very depth of your being. Country is going to church in a little brick schoolhouse because the big church downtown felt too uptown. Country is picking from a small patch of wild blackberries growing alongside a creek not too far from your subdivision and bringing them home to Mama, then kicking back and soaking in the smell of her homemade blackberry cobbler drifting from the oven. The leftover berries, of course, were shared with the folks next door.

I don't remember Daddy locking our doors at night. I do remember shelling peas on the screened porch, adopting and loving a little black dog that wandered into our yard late one afternoon, and lying in bed at night listening to the *Grand Ole Opry* on my radio with the music of cool Southern raindrops bouncing off the tin roof outside.

Yep, I grew up country in the city. And I wouldn't trade my raisin' for anything in the world.

Troy Gentry

Where music and life intersect, that's where you'll find Troy Gentry. As half of the multiplatinum duo Montgomery Gentry, the northern Kentucky native has been one of country music's most popular young performers of recent years, racking up hit after hit with his bandmate, Eddie Montgomery. Growing up, Troy developed a love for acts like Elvis, George Jones, Bruce Springsteen, Merle Haggard, and Randy Travis as he and his mother sang along to the records. Like Eddie, Troy spent as much time in honky-tonks as he did in school. The two first started playing music together with Eddie's older brother John Michael, but became a duo when he left to pursue a solo career. Their raw, tell-it-like-it-is approach has hit a home run with music fans who like their musicians free from a manufactured corporate gloss. As Troy tells it, "We still look at life the same way we did when we were working two jobs and playing music at night in the clubs to make ends meet." In 2000, they cleaned up on the awards circuit with a Country Music Association Vocal Duo of the Year Award, the American Music Award for Favorite New Artist—Country, and the Academy of Country Music's award for Top New Vocal Group or Duo. Their greatest-hits album, *Something to Be Proud Of*, was released in 2005.

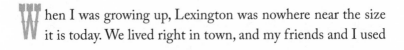 hen I was growing up, Lexington was nowhere near the size it is today. We lived right in town, and my friends and I used

to sneak onto the golf course behind our house. We played cowboys and Indians in between the sand traps and wooded areas. My street was full of friends, and we spent hours outside playing anything we could think of. Back then, there was so much to do around my house that we didn't need to venture into any mischief or any kind of trouble.

My family was a *Hee Haw* family—we'd sit down and watch it on Sunday nights. Mom loved watching the awards shows to see her favorite singers, and she always had records playing in our house. Seeing all those stars in the limelight, all the glitz and glamour, rubbed off on me. My little brother, a couple friends, and I used to put on mini-concerts in our backyard. We beat on the pots and pans from the kitchen and the plastic guitars we bought at the store. A turntable would spin a record, and we'd pantomime the whole album. I think we even charged admission one time. These days, my concerts are a little different, but I still just want to have a good time. Eddie and I have always wanted to make music about everyday life whether it be good or bad—music that people could embrace. We want people to hear our song "Lonely and Gone" and have it help them when they are going through a hard time. We want people to know that they're not alone. Or when they listen to "Hell Yeah," we want them to celebrate a hard week of work. People work so hard to make ends meet, to raise a family, to try to do right. Everybody, regardless of how much they get caught up in their work, needs some time to let off steam—to be able to relax, let their hair down, forget their cares and worries, and go "hell yeah!" We're all the same people fighting and struggling to do something good in life. Just don't forget to let go and have a good time.

Bill Kirchen

The Grammy-nominated guitarist, singer, and songwriter Bill Kirchen can step onto any stage, rip into his trademark licks, and leave the audience quaking in their shoes. In a career that spans over thirty years, Bill, with his guitar prowess, has shared the stage with some of the most esteemed artists of his day, including Emmylou Harris, Elvis Costello, and Nick Lowe. Labeled a "Titan of the Telecaster" by *Guitar Player* magazine, Bill has come a long way since jamming with his college buddies in Michigan. In 1969, he convinced his Commander Cody and His Lost Planet Airmen bandmates to move out to California, where they set up shop in San Francisco during the legendary psychedelic era. Soon, the hard-rocking, genre-crisscrossing band was garnering praise from all corners of the music landscape. Truckers, frat boys, pot smokers, and cowboys showed up in droves to catch their shows. For years, the band set out in their secondhand Greyhound bus and toured the nation, defying any attempt to classify their truly original sound and picking up scores of fans in every city they burst into. After the band broke up, Bill moved between San Francisco, Ann Arbor, Austin, and Washington, D.C., collaborating with different musicians in every locale. His latest album, *Dieselbilly Road Trip*, is a musical travelogue of sorts, with songs inspired by city stops all over the United States.

've been a folk music fan ever since the sixties. I was at the Newport Folk Festival in 1964 and '65 and saw tons of bluegrass,

string band, gospel, and blues—even Bob Dylan going electric—
but until we got together as Commander Cody and His Lost
Planet Airmen, I had heard very little electric country music,
meaning the commercial country of the forties, fifties, and sixties.
Billy C. Farlow and John Tichy already knew a whole bunch of
the songs and history, so along with the records we were finding
in the $1.98 cut-out bins, I got a crash course in hard-core coun-
try and rockabilly.

I got right into it. I've never turned my back on rock 'n' roll; I
played it then and I play it now, but country had adult themes and
a musical vibe that grabbed me. The players were great, hotter
than some of the rock and rollers I had been listening to. The
sound of those Capitol records by Buck Owens, Tommy Collins,
Merle Haggard, and Red Simpson, along with the rockabilly and
western swing I was hearing, just knocked me out. I went out and
got myself a Telecaster as fast as I could.

I packed up my gear in Ann Arbor, moved to San Francisco in
1969, and dragged the rest of the band out later that year. That
was where things were happening, and I had to be there. We
ended up being Gene Vincent's band for a week, Emmylou Harris's band for a month, and Doug Kershaw's for a long weekend. I
sold a motorcycle for the rent on a band house, we ate scavenged
groceries, and in less than a year we were up and running.

We were listening to tons of Hank Williams, Ernest Tubb,
and Lefty Frizzell, and we were hell-bent on playing real blood-
and-guts country. I remember getting a lecture early on from a
member of the Grateful Dead who shall remain nameless (it
wasn't Jerry) right after we opened a show for them in San Francisco. He took me aside and said, "You really should update your
tonalities." He proceeded to give me a demonstration of how to
sing Haggard's "Mama Tried" in the "new" way, kind of high-
pitched and drawn-out. Of course, he was well-meaning, but I

thought it was hilarious. Our plan was to get back to an original rootsy rocking sound, and "update your tonalities" became a derogatory catchphrase for us for years to come.

We hit the road hard. With eight band members, four roadies, and all of our equipment crammed into an old Greyhound bus we'd bought in Nashville, we were out for 250 days a year. We took a page from the country and soul guys by using a tour bus. None of the West Coast rock bands were doing it at the time. I will say that we had way more fun than we deserved. Crossing back and forth between the rock and country scenes was an adventure. We had been putting out singles on Paramount, including our Top 10 hit "Hot Rod Lincoln," and they decided to also release our more country efforts on their Nashville-based Dot label, even though we were less than country–looking hippies. We played the huge DJ Convention (now known as Fan Fair) with hair flying everywhere. There was some snickering and the announcer made a semi-snide remark, but as soon as we broke out with "Diggy Diggy Lo," everything was cool. You could almost see the thought balloons above the crowd's head: *Not bad for some long-haired hippie freaks.*

We eventually pushed the limits too far for Nashville. We were doing okay until our third album. We had gotten our hands on an old western swing record by the Modern Mountaineers called "Everybody's Truckin'," which supposedly featured the F-word. Their record slurred the word "truckin'" just enough to make it sound like the non-airplay-friendly word, but you really couldn't hear it clearly. Well, we decided to remove any doubt when we cut the song. We used the rhyming word about eighty times in that one song. Pulling something like that was unheard of in 1973, but it didn't end there. Paramount put out the record with a disclaimer across the front: "Cut 3, Side 2: Not Suitable for Airplay." Now, to this day, I don't know if it was just dumb luck or somebody at the record company playing a practical joke, but cut 3 on side 2 wasn't the problem song. Our version, "Everybody's Doin' It," hit the radio stations unprotected, while the song with the "Not Suitable" tag was our one gospel song. Uh-oh. Dot Records dropped us like a bad habit with a letter that began, "Gentlemen, we have a serious problem here." We thought country music was big and ugly enough to handle something like that, but we were wrong. That was the end of Commander Cody on country radio for many years.

Stoney LaRue

Some three-year-olds play with blocks and toy cars. Others belt out renditions of John Anderson's "Swingin'" on a Mr. Microphone radio. Put the mesmerizing performer Stoney LaRue in the latter category. Born in Texas and raised in Oklahoma, Stoney was a natural-born performer who listened to everything from Willie Nelson to the Grateful Dead. With a burning desire to feed his music muse, Stoney packed up and headed to the hotbed of Stillwater, where the Red Dirt movement was gaining momentum and churning out fresh and raw music. In 2002, he teamed up with the Organic Boogie Band to release "Downtown." Recorded in the renowned Tulsa ballroom Cain's and mixed in a trailer, the song was fused with Red Dirt vibes. The good feedback on "Downtown" inspired him to move to New Braunfels, Texas, where he found a vibrant music community that embraced him. In 2005, his *Red Dirt Album* made it to the *Billboard* charts during the first week it was released. With an unquenchable desire for sharing the music that fills his soul, Stoney performs close to three hundred dates a year with acts such as Lee Ann Womack, Radney Foster, and Dierks Bentley.

Growing up country means waking up early, working in the garden, eating lunch, going fishing down at the old *crick*, eating dinner, working in the garden some more, then spending the rest of the evening sitting on the front porch. I feel blessed to have grown up in the country, and I can see it in my music. When I was ten years old, I picked up an acoustic guitar. My brother Bo had gotten a guitar for his birthday, and I really, really wanted to play guitar. I just wanted an outlet to express myself creatively, so I played anywhere I could—local contests, 4-H shows, Future Farmers of America events. The first time I played in a bar was when I played with my dad. After the show, I got a dollar. I told myself I was going to save it, but of course, I went out and spent it immediately.

Country is an attitude. Mixing "Downtown" in a trailer perched on a cliff in Oklahoma with a bunch of older and incredibly talented musicians, man, that was *country*. We were getting back to our roots, putting our heart into it. We were making music the way it should be made—for the pure love of it, not for a big recording contract. We were surrounded by a raw power I could feel down to my bones. It isn't just something you listen to. It's a way of life. A certain set of values. It's Red Dirt Music, and that's a banner I'm proud to wave.

Sherwin Linton

After fifty years of electrifying performances and with five thousand songs in his repertoire, Sherwin Linton shows no sign of slowing down. Growing up in South Dakota, he spent his days strumming the guitar and working out the chords to his favorite songs on the piano. At sixteen, Sherwin scored his own show on the local KWAT radio station. After playing in nightclubs and ballrooms across the country with the Fender Benders, he journeyed to Nashville and cut "Cotton King," a song that soared to the top of the country charts. In 1971, Sherwin took his deep, resonating voice behind the granite walls of the South Dakota State Penitentiary and hammered out the original tribute to the Man in Black. That live album, *Hello, I'm Not Johnny Cash*, catapulted Sherwin back to the top, earning him two consecutive nominations for the Country Music Association's Entertainer of the Year Award. With an infectious smile and humble humor, Sherwin plays 250 dates a year and continues to win over fans of all ages. Braving blizzards, tornadoes, and floods, this tireless performer was even recognized by *Ripley's Believe It or Not* for the amazing feat of never missing a performance during his career. "I thank God for what he's given me, and feel the best is yet to come." His latest albums include *It Happened in America*, released in 2003, and 2005's *Dakota Railroad Town Centennial*.

Back in 1944, we lived in the little town of Osceola, South Dakota (population: 25), where my dad was a section foreman on the Great Northern Railway. Our house was about fifty feet from the railroad track. The railroad provided what they called a section house for the section foreman to live in. We moved around quite a lot, because my dad worked different jobs all over the railroad line, and in every small town we moved to, our house was on one side of the track and the rest of the town was on the other. We usually had pasture or farmland directly behind our home, and my dad, who loved to garden, had a few acres of railroad right-of-way that we would use to plant his vegetables. There was a railroad water tower directly across from our house that held the water the trains would take on to produce steam. The tank on that water tower was about fifteen, maybe even twenty, feet in diameter—it was a pretty big tank—and at least ten feet deep. When I was four years old, my brother, who was eleven years older than me, took me up the ladder to the roof of that water tower. We went through a trapdoor and then down another ladder into the water. It was down in there that my brother taught me how to float, so I got my first swimming lesson in a railroad water tower.

My music roots and my country roots are inseparable. Most country homes had music inside of them. At least half had a piano—even people of minimal means managed to have one. It was the main source of entertainment. I remember sitting at the piano when I was five years old, plunking away at "The Caissons Go Rolling Along," a popular song from World War II. I also played a "paper and a comb." This was done by using wax-covered bread-wrapper paper and holding it against a comb, then humming onto the paper with your lips. This would produce musical sounds much like those of a kazoo. When I was six, my brother brought home a little windup, portable phonograph. He worked on the railroad in high school, and he had bought it for about four dollars from somebody he worked with. I'd open the phonograph, wind it up, and put old 78 records on. On the inside of the cover, a picture of the Sons of the Pioneers was thumbtacked. One of my favorite records was by Bob Wills and His Texas Playboys. I played "Spanish Two Step" over and over, wondering what it would be like down below the Rio Grande. "Down below the Rio Grande / Señorita held my hand." Inspired by the Sons of the Pioneers picture, I fastened a ruler to an old cigar box, put rubber bands around it, and suddenly I had a little guitar! It wasn't tunable, but it made me happy just the same. When I was ten, a man who worked with my father on the railroad and who had a couple of guitars showed me the chords he knew. Shortly after that, I was singing at community events and on the radio, so that was the real beginning of my own musical career.

Music seeped into every part of my life in the country. Some of the best times were spent on Sunday afternoons taking leisurely drives with my parents, rambling down those gravel roads, looking at the countryside, while Dad sang old songs from his younger days and my mother played her double-reed harmonica. We didn't have a radio, but by my memory their music was the best I've ever heard.

Gary Rossington

A founding member and guitarist of the legendary Southern rock band Lynyrd Skynyrd, Gary Rossington fell in love with music when he saw the Beatles on *The Ed Sullivan Show*. Determined to buy a guitar, he got a paper route and collected Coke bottles and scrap metal to finance his new dream. As soon as he had enough money in his pocket, he put down a deposit on a sixty-dollar Sears Silvertone guitar. Then, one day in 1964, history was made when thirteen-year-old Gary and his friends decided to form a band. Not being able to get through a single song during their first rehearsal didn't matter. Lynyrd Skynyrd was born. The band received national exposure in 1973 with the release of their first album and hit single, "Free Bird." Platinum albums and hit songs like "Sweet Home Alabama," "Saturday Night Special," "Gimme Back My Bullets," and "That Smell" quickly catapulted the band into rock-star status. Tragedy struck in 1977 when a plane crash killed three of the group's members and the road manager and left the rest of the band and crew seriously injured. In 1991, after many years of recovery, soul-searching, and playing with different bands, Gary and a re-formed Lynyrd Skynyrd emerged with the first new material in fourteen years. Since then, the band has crisscrossed America and Europe playing to sold-out crowds at every stop. In 2006, the multiplatinum band was inducted into the Rock and Roll Hall of Fame. With his usual grace and genuine gratitude, Gary called it "a humbling honor."

acksonville, Florida—what a great place to grow up. Back then, there were so many rivers and creeks and lakes to explore. I used to play hooky with my friends so we could spend all day fishing. The west side of Cedar Hills in Jacksonville during the late 1950s and early 1960s was a lot like *The Andy Griffith Show*. Back in those days, you'd wake up, put your shorts on, and run outside. Kids never bothered to put on shoes or shirts. Sunday was the only day I wasn't playing outside. I was raised Catholic, so every Sunday I was in church instead of running around with my friends. I used to get mad at my mother since most kids were playing baseball or football and I wanted to be out there instead of at Sunday school, but now I'm so grateful I was raised with the Lord. I have him in my heart and soul, and I thank him every day for still having me here.

My father died when I was young, so I was a real mama's boy. I didn't cuss or drink or get into trouble. At least not until I was in my late teens. Until then, I was a good boy. And I knew from a young age that I wanted to play music. Around my town, there were a lot of people who played acoustic guitars and country music. There was a place called Pritchett's Kitchen on Cedar Creek that had a fish fry every Saturday afternoon. Great country acts like Jimmy Strickland, Glenn Reeves, and Shorty Medlocke used to go there to jam. When we were little, we'd go with our parents, and when we got a little older, we'd ride our bikes there on our own. That's when you start hearing all the old men telling their stories about hunting and fishing, most of which were exaggerated of course. Back in those days it was a whole neighborhood, a whole village that raised the kids. It was a different time.

I was a huge Elvis fan. I remember coming home from seeing *Jailhouse Rock* at the theater and spending hours in front of my mirror with a broom for a microphone, trying to dance and sing like he did. A friend of mine had a set of drums and he could keep a beat, and I thought he was the coolest kid in town. He taught me to play a little bit, and I'd go to his house every other day, but after a while when I saw guitar players, I just fell in love with them. When I was ten years old, I decided the guitar was for me. Ricky Nelson and Fabian were so cool. Then I graduated up to the blues and Chuck Berry. I loved all the blues and country musicians on the *Grand Ole Opry*. Hearing the different pickers, banjos, slide players, and steel guitars, I was just amazed. It wasn't the singing as much as the playing. Then, when I was thirteen years old, I saw the Beatles on *The Ed Sullivan Show*. Right then, I knew I wanted to be in a band.

My friends and I used to spend a lot of time playing Little League baseball. One day Ronnie Van Zant's team was playing, and Bob Burns and I were hanging out watching the game. All of a sudden Ronnie hit a foul ball that came straight for Bob's head, even knocked him out for a second. That's how we all met. After that game, the three of us started talking about music. I had a guitar and a little bitty nothing of a Silvertone amp, Bob had a set of drums, and Ronnie sang. The next day we met at Bob's house and started playing together. Back then, Ronnie had a badass, roughneck reputation. He was always getting in fights, most of which he won.

Allen Collins went to school with us, and we heard he had a guitar and amp, so we tried to round him up for the band, too. One day we were driving around in Ronnie's 1965 Mustang, and we saw Allen riding his bike. We tried to call him over to the car, but as soon as he saw we were with Ronnie, he figured we were going to beat him up, so he went flying off into the woods. We had to chase him down, and we finally found him hiding up in a tree. It took a while to convince him we just wanted to talk to him about being in our band. Finally he believed us and came down from the tree, and we headed to his house to pick up his guitar and amp. And that's how Lynyrd Skynyrd started.

Being a rock star doesn't really mean anything. To me, stars are things that are up in the sky. Being a good person is what really matters. Spending time with family and friends and enjoying good old Southern hospitality are what bring me happiness now. There is something special about living down South. People are real down here. All my friends, no matter what they do for a living—truck drivers, gardeners, construction workers—are proud of who they are. People look you in the eye down here. The spirit of community is in your heart. You are just born that way. I love it down South, and I'll always be here.

Donnie Van Zant

The son of a hardworking truck driver, Donnie Van Zant grew up in a home full of Merle Haggard, Hank Williams, and Mel Tillis records. Music seeped into the Van Zant boys' blood early on. Donnie is the younger brother of the Lynyrd Skynyrd founding member and singer, Ronnie Van Zant, and the older brother of the Southern rock singer Johnny Van Zant. In 1975, Donnie formed 38 Special and took on the role of lead singer. Originally a Southern rock band, they took on a harder rock edge, resulting in over a dozen hit singles, including "Hold On Loosely," "Caught Up in You," "If I'd Been the One," and "Second Chance." The multiplatinum group continues to pack stadiums and released their latest album, *Drivetrain*, in 2004. Known for his unflagging energy, Donnie has recently returned to his country roots. His long-awaited musical collaboration with his younger brother, Johnny, as Van Zant is the fulfillment of a promise he made to himself after his older brother, Ronnie, was tragically killed in a 1977 plane crash. Extolling working-class values, their album, *Get Right with the Man*, was a smash right out of the gate. With the multiple-week Top 10 single "Help Somebody," the album had the distinction of being the highest-selling debut country album in 2005. Blurring the traditional boundaries between country and rock and roll, Donnie's latest efforts have further solidified the Van Zants as Southern rock's first family.

The west side of Jacksonville, Florida, was nicknamed Shanty-town. In a ramshackle neighborhood with a constant police presence, there was definitely some moonshining going on. I can see now that we were poor, but we didn't know that at the time. My mother and father kept clothes on our backs and food on the table. The one thing that I always knew we had in our home was love, and that was the most important thing to us.

There was never a dull moment in the Van Zant home. My father was a long-distance truck driver and wasn't home all that often, so my mother was both Mom and Dad to us six kids—myself, two brothers, and three sisters. We definitely kept her hands full growing up, but she obviously knew what she was doing: most of our friends from childhood ended up either in jail or dead. Family has everything to do with how I survived and what I've accomplished with my life and my career.

Growing up when I did was just totally different from growing up today. Instead of PlayStations and the Internet, we had bamboo and string. We would make a bow and arrows out of that, and then let our imaginations run wild. We would pretend we were Daniel Boone or Davy Crockett. If we could talk our mother out of an old bedsheet, we'd rip it in half, draw a big old *S* on it, and we had a Superman outfit. Our imaginations were our entertainment.

Music became a part of our lives at an early age. We had a piano in the house, and we all played around on it. We didn't take it very seriously at first; music was just a part of our household and a part of where we came from. I can remember watching Ronnie rehearse in my mother and father's living room. At that time, his group was called One Percent. Here I was just a little guy with a butch haircut watching them rehearse and thinking,

Man, they are having a great time here. Maybe I can do this! That's probably the reason I got into the music business, to be more like my big brother.

Music for me is a simple, honest thing—I'm an expert on the G, E, A, and C chords! You can write so many songs with those four chords. One of the many lessons that Ronnie taught me was that you write songs to move people emotionally and spiritually. If you can do that, you've won. Ronnie showed me that honesty and communication of real experience are what songwriting is all about, and I have tried to write and live by his example throughout my career. Make-believe was important to us growing up, but only honesty matters in music.

Music and family are inseparable to me at this point. Performing with my brother Johnny is an unbelievable feeling. We both have the attitude to just go out there onstage and have fun, which is how we learned to play music in the first place. A lot of musicians today take music and themselves a little too seriously and forget why they started playing in the first place—to communicate honestly with the audience, and to have fun doing it. It means a whole lot to Johnny and me that we get to make music together now, but even more important is that we just get to be together.

My father passed away in 2005, so I don't return to my childhood home very often. But it will always be a part of me and will always influence everything I do. I may have moved away from home in body, but I never could in spirit or in values. And when I say moved away, I'm talking about fifteen miles—so I didn't end up getting too far anyway!

HOME

Rhett Akins

A Georgia boy through and through, Rhett Akins went away to college with little more than his cowboy boots and guitars. After his football-playing days for the Georgia Bulldogs came to an end, he left school with one mission: to make it in Nashville. Since then, Rhett has become one of the most-talked-about young country artists with a string of hits, including his No. I songs, "That Ain't My Truck" and "Don't Get Me Started," the Top 10 "She Said Yes," and his new controversial song, "Kiss My Country Ass." A hard-core outdoorsman and loving father, Rhett has a talent for expressing life as the quintessential everyman that makes him a roaring crowd favorite. Rhett's honesty just pours out of his music. Of his songwriting, he says, "There is no filter in between what I want to say and what goes on paper." Rhett has been touring for the past eleven years, singing his Southern-inspired songs to millions of people all across the United States. His latest album on BNA Records, *People Like Me*, focuses on what he knows best—music, family, and the great outdoors.

ncle Charles, Uncle Charles . . . Help!" I screamed as I ran into my uncle's house in the middle of the night, hoping he'd somehow get us out of trouble without letting my dad or granddad know about it. Not this time—this problem was too big. The entire family was bound to find out.

A couple of buddies and I had camped out on our farm, and we wanted to build a fire. We tried and we tried to get the wood to start burning, but it just wouldn't light. Not using much (okay, any) common sense, we grabbed some bales of hay, which lit instantly. We were out in the middle of a field at the height of a dry summer—not a good combination. The fire started spreading and we did everything we could to stop it, but it spread faster than we could stamp it out. Finally I had to run and get Uncle Charles, the go-to guy whenever I got myself into a bad situation. He got the tractor and the backhoe and dug trenches all around the fire so it would stop—we literally almost burned the farm down.

I grew up on a five-hundred-acre farm, and my whole family—aunts, uncles, cousins, and grandparents—all lived within shouting distance on the property. It was like the Waltons. We had horses running around, peach orchards, fishing ponds, a runway for my granddad's Beechcraft Bonanza and Cessna planes (which made the trip to Georgia football games a lot faster), and miles of trails to ride our motorcycles and four-wheelers on. We even built an enormous tree house in a huge live oak tree. It was like something straight out of a movie—branches hanging down to the ground and Spanish moss hanging off of them—that my buddies and I hung out in for years. It was *the* place for all my friends to hang out at, which also meant there were plenty of opportunities to call Uncle Charles to help us out when we were in over our heads.

We had a couple of old, beat-up farm trucks sitting on our property that we used for hauling trash and loading lumber. There was this little blue Datsun that ended up in that junk car pile, but it still ran. One night me and my buddy (the same one from the almost-burned-down-the-farm incident) decided to take the little car out to the river. We'd had a lot of rain, and the river had overflowed, so there was this whole area of the woods that stayed wet and just full of mud. We had to get through that patch on our way to the river, so we headed for it at about eighty miles an hour. We held our breath as we approached, but the Datsun made it across!

We hung out at the river shooting fireworks for a while, and then decided to make the journey home. We headed for that pile of mud at a pretty good clip but weren't as lucky as the first time. The front tire went down into a huge rut, and we completely flipped over onto our side, leaving us crammed against the passenger door. We were scared to death. We managed to climb out of the car, and we tried our best to flip it back, but it wouldn't even budge. It was one o'clock in the morning, we were getting killed by mosquitoes—Georgia's are the worst in the world—and we had to walk all the way back to the house in the pitch black, dodging water moccasins and rattlesnakes. Once we got home, we didn't want to tell a soul, so we quietly snuck our four-wheelers out and didn't crank them until we were a good distance from the house. We got back to the car, tied some ropes to it, gunned our four-wheelers, and somehow managed to get the car back on its wheels. But we still couldn't start it up. Three hours later, we're knocking on Uncle Charles's door, begging him to help us. Again. He got on his tractor, drove out to the river at four o'clock in the morning, and pulled that Datsun right out of the mud. My friends started calling Uncle Charles "Jama Man" because the only time they saw him he was stumbling out of his house, half-asleep with his pajamas on, cursing the latest trouble we'd gotten into, even as he was helping us get out of it.

I've lived in Nashville for years now, but I still love going back to the farm. I feel like a fish going back to the water as soon as I step foot on that land. It just feels natural. The times I spent on our farm are some of the best times of my life. Nowadays, my kids can't wait to go there every summer, and they get into *exactly* the same trouble I did—and we still call on Jama Man to come to the rescue.

Deborah Allen

Working as a waitress isn't usually at the top of a singer's list. But in Deborah Allen's case, her days at a Nashville pancake house were her big break. While waiting on Roy Orbison, she convinced him to hire her as a backup singer. She made ninety dollars in one session—she was as excited as if it had been a million. After cutting her teeth at Opryland and touring the world with Tennessee Ernie Ford, the Memphis native returned to Nashville brimming with the confidence to take her career to the next level. A meeting with Jim Stafford led to a move to Los Angeles, where Deborah worked with Jim on television and opened for him in concert. Two years was enough in the land of sunshine, and she headed back to Nashville to focus her energy on singing and songwriting. She was handpicked by Jim Reeves's widow to complete the unfinished vocal duets he left behind, including the hits "Oh, How I Miss You Tonight" and "Take Me in Your Arms and Hold Me," both of which shot to the top of the charts. Through the 1980s and 1990s, Deborah's prolific work produced hit after hit, including her signature songs, "Baby I Lied," "I Hurt for You," "Rock Me," and "If You're Not Gonna Love Me." And her work just keeps getting better. Now, along with her myriad awards and Grammy nominations as a recording artist and songwriter, Deborah has gone on to become a distinguished member of BMI's Million-Air club with songs recorded by LeAnn Rimes, Patty Loveless, Janie Fricke, John Conlee, Fleetwood Mac, Diana Ross, George Jones, Conway Twitty, and Loretta Lynn. Most recently, Deborah scored multiplatinum status as a writer when her song

"We Can Get There," recorded by the pop diva Mary Griffin, appeared on the *Coyote Ugly* sound track.

> *Two young lovers on a Blytheville back road*
> *Layin' on the levee makin' love all night long*
> *Wishin' on a star in a southern sky*
> *Dreamin' out loud about the rest of their lives*
> *They were lost, . . . lost in love*
> *In a Delta Dreamland.*

I grew up going to work every day with my mother, who helped out at my daddy's automobile upholstery and detail shop in Memphis, Tennessee. I was greeting the public at a very early age and loved hangin' out with the colorful mix of employees.

But one of the most fun things I used to look forward to as a little girl was when our family would load up and take a drive over the Memphis-Arkansas Bridge, heading on to Blytheville to my grandmother and granddaddy Posey's house. That is also where my mother and daddy, Rosetta and Leon, met and fell in love, and later it became the inspiration for my song "Delta Dreamland."

Grandmother and Granddaddy's place was just a little country house with brownish brick-looking siding. It looked like roofing to me. The yard had big shade trees, and the driveway was kind of soft, sandy dirt.

My two sisters, Nancy and Judy, and I, along with my cousins, used to take sticks and draw hopscotch boards in the sandy dirt driveway. We would laugh and play all day. Sometimes, on a sweltering summer day, Judy and I would get a shovel and tell Grandmother we were going out in the cotton field that backed up to the train track behind her house to "dig." We were going to see if we could dig to China. Grandmother was always agreeable, but would warn us not to go too far out in the field, because sometimes some of "those old hoboes" who rode the trains might be out there and might "get us!" That added an exciting sense of danger to our international diggin' mission.

I always loved the big family gatherings when all the aunts and uncles would come with our cousins and we would play outside all day. It was the epitome of good country livin'. There was a rooster and chickens with eggs in the henhouse. There was always an old dog hangin' round. There were pots under the bed for those cold winter nights when you didn't want to make the trip to the outhouse. There were roll-away beds to make due for all the company. And there was plenty of good food. Grandmother was a really great country cook, and she taught her daughters well.

When I was around two or three years old, I climbed up on the kitchen table while Grandmother and my mother were cookin' a big dinner. While their backs were turned, I ate a whole huge bowl of cold pork 'n' beans before they knew it. I didn't get in trouble. It gave everyone a big laugh. It gave me a big bellyache, but, oh, how I still love pork 'n' beans!

At night I used to love to lie between my mother and my daddy on those cool sheets in that back bedroom. I felt so safe, happy, and loved. I'd flop one leg over each of their legs and lay one arm on each of them to make sure I was spreadin' my love evenly to them. I loved to hear them talkin' as I stared up at the bare lightbulb in the ceiling. Then, when the lights went out, I would ask them, "What are those lights out there?" They would tell me it was the interstate with truckers and all kinds of people travelin' all over the world. I would imagine traveling those roads, not knowing at the time that my music would be the vehicle that would take me on that journey.

I love my childhood memories of my grandparents' house in Blytheville; even then it felt as if being there was like being closer to heaven. Time moved slower, making it easier to soak up the magic of each moment.

These days, when the world gets too busy, I let my mind drift back to my Delta Dreamland.

Johnny Bush

Entering his fifth decade of performing, Johnny Bush is truly a master in country music. Raised in a rough, blue-collar Houston neighborhood, Johnny got his start as a teenager in the house band at San Antonio's Texas Star Inn before joining Willie Nelson's band the Record Men, and later Ray Price's Cherokee Cowboys. In 1967, he scored his first hit with "You Ought to Hear Me Cry," and in 1972 his song "Whiskey River" (which would eventually become Nelson's signature song) hit the Top 10. In the early 1970s, Johnny faced a singer's worst nightmare when he suddenly experienced a tightness in his voice. The unexplained vocal troubles escalated until he could not even talk. After six frustrating and heartbreaking years in search of an answer, Johnny was finally diagnosed with spastic dysphonia, a disorder that caused uncontrollable spasms in his vocal cords. He has since become an advocate for those afflicted with the disease, and, thanks to his courageous and determined search for treatment, he has been able to regain most of his vocal ability. With the release of 1994's Western swing album *Time Changes Everything*, Johnny's career entered a renaissance, and his hard-core honky-tonk sound found a new generation of fans. In 2004 he released *Honky Tonic*, which contains his never-before-recorded duet version of "Whiskey River" with Nelson, and in 2006 the prolific musician released the album *Texas State of Mind*. The Texas Country Music Hall of Famer is also the author of *Whiskey River Take My Mind: The True Story of the Texas Honky-Tonk* (2007).

Kashmere Gardens was an obscure part of Houston north of Buffalo Bayou where, back in the 1920s, they tried to grow cotton along the banks. My grandfather bought some lots, and we all moved into the three-room shotgun house he built himself. You could look out the kitchen door to the southwest and see the skyline of Houston seven and a half miles away. But being close enough to see Houston certainly didn't mean we had the conveniences of Houston. We had no running water, gas, or electricity in our house. There were chickens running around in the yard, and the only restroom was an outhouse—Grandma called it the "relief office." Growing up, we had no idea we were poor—everybody lived just like we did out there.

For entertainment, my dad built us a little crystal radio set. My brother and I could listen at the same time through one set of split earphones. As you searched around on this crystal with a needle, you could pick up different radio stations. We listened, like everyone else in those days, to the *Grand Ole Opry*.

Around 1943, my dad got an old car that had a radio in it. As soon as he'd come home from work, I'd go out in the parked car and listen to all those wonderful old programs like *Jack Armstrong*, *Terry and the Pirates*, *Captain Midnight*, and *The Jack Benny Show*. I learned to use my imagination by listening to the shows, creating the story to go along with the sounds coming from the speakers.

My dad belonged to the National Guard, so once a week he had to go to the Armory. The Armory was located in a ritzy part of town. To me, ritzy was a place with paved streets, sidewalks, and manicured lawns, things that we were not used to seeing at all. In our neighborhood, the old gray gumbo mud constantly covered our shoes and the bottoms of our pant legs. I was kind of ashamed when we would go somewhere like the Armory and see that there was a better life out there than the one we were living. But one thing we didn't lack in our house was love. My mom was a great cook, and she also made all of our clothes by hand out of feed sacks and flour sacks. While I was jealous of those who lived in better neighborhoods, I was also proud of our handmade clothes and the abundance of warmth and togetherness that defined our family.

My other glimpse into the ritzy world was going to movies for the Saturday matinees. My heroes, like everyone else's at the time, were Gene Autry and Roy Rogers, the singing cowboys. By the age of twelve, I was a regular on a live radio show on KTHT (the station is still on the air). My brother, who was nine, and I did a Homer and Jethro act every Monday night. One evening, Gene Autry walked into the station. I couldn't believe it. The rodeo was in town, so he came into the station for a promotional live appearance. In awe when I was introduced to him, the only thing I could think to ask was, "How's Champion?" That was his horse, and in those days the cowboy's horse was as important to us as the actor was. "Champion's fine," he said. "If you come down, I'll let you ride him." I couldn't believe it! We showed up at the rodeo, but I couldn't find Mr. Autry or Champion anywhere. Of course, our tickets were so high up I nearly got a nosebleed, so finding Champion would have been pretty difficult. For years since that day, I have had vivid dreams of taking that ride.

My dad gave me a little three-quarter-sized guitar when I was ten years old and taught me a few chords. That was our entertainment when there was no radio. Playing and singing while we sat on the porch—people actually sat on porches back in those days—with Granddad on the fiddle and Dad on the guitar. I still remember, will always remember, those old songs—"Pistol Packin' Mama" and "She'll Be Comin' 'Round the Mountain." Some of Dad's musician friends stopped in from time to time. While the other kids were outside playing ball or going down to the woods, I'd be sitting on the porch watching their fingers make chords, listening to the wonderful music being played.

I definitely grew up country, but it was in the city. That was the difference. I didn't look out my back door to see crops growing. By today's standards—even by the standards back then—we were considered white trash, definitely among the have-nots, but that kind of life made me who I am. My love for music started on that little crystal radio, letting my imagination run wild. We provided our own entertainment—the best music was the kind we made ourselves, out on the porch as the sun was setting, surrounded by friends and family and loving every minute of it.

{ President Jimmy } Carter

James Earl Carter Jr., the thirty-ninth president of the United States, grew up in a tiny farming community in Plains, Georgia. Peanut farming, talk of politics, and devotion to the Baptist faith formed the backbone of his upbringing. After graduating from the United States Naval Academy, Jimmy Carter became a submariner, serving in both the Atlantic and the Pacific fleets. When his father died in 1953, his life path led him back to his tiny hometown. As the oldest of four children, Carter resigned his naval commission so he could return home to take over his family's farms. With his inimitable Southern charm and genuine devotion to public welfare, he quickly became a leader in the community and rose in the political ranks. During his presidency, his major accomplishments included the creation of a national energy policy and the consolidation of governmental agencies. He enacted strong environmental legislation, deregulated the trucking, airline, rail, finance, communications, and oil industries, bolstered the social security system, and appointed record numbers of women and minorities to significant government and judicial posts. Since leaving office, Carter has served as an international mediator, traveling extensively to monitor elections, conduct peace negotiations, and establish relief efforts. In 2002, he won the Nobel Peace Prize. A true Southerner, he continues to make his home in Plains, Georgia.

I was born and raised in the country, and each year my love for rural life has been strengthened. I could have lived anywhere after being governor and president, but I have always chosen to move back where our family first settled more than 170 years ago. One of the things I like most about country life is that nothing much has really changed. The best of modern times can be melded into the finest aspects of days gone by. Country Music Television on a wide plasma screen has replaced the sometimes weak and scratchy sounds of the *Grand Ole Opry* coming from our battery radio, but the innate personal pleasure from the music is still there. My grandchildren and I are still walking and hunting in the same woods and fishing in the same creeks as I did with my father. We still have some of the same neighbors and younger ones just like us who worship, play, and work together as always.

When we leave our little town of Plains and the 634 people who live there, we can drive to Atlanta stock-car races, to symphony concerts, or to see the Braves or Falcons play ball. We can still make it back home in time to go to bed—in the country.

Ralph Emery

A legendary DJ and television host in Nashville, Ralph Emery has been witness to some of the best American country music from the 1960s through today. Beginning his career when he was just eighteen years old, Ralph knocked around various stations until landing at Nashville's AM WSM seven years later. As the all-night disc jockey for fifteen years, he hosted a popular late-night show that attracted country musicians of all sorts, in particular Tex Ritter, whose co-hosting appearances in 1966 and 1967 made for legendary shows. After a year and a half of hilarious and unforgettable broadcasts, Tex's radio duties came to an end when his wife, Dorothy, decided she wanted him home when he wasn't on the road. Ralph's show continued to be a favorite of country music fans and stars alike, including Merle Haggard, Loretta Lynn, and Marty Robbins. Often his interviews turned into extended late-night impromptu jam sessions, much to the delight of the legions of overnight long-haul truck drivers who faithfully listened to his show. With Ralph at the helm, country music was shared from coast to coast and gained countless new fans. From 1974 to 1980, he hosted a nationally syndicated music show, *Pop! Goes the Country*, and from 1983 to 1993 he hosted *Nashville Now* on the Nashville Network, bringing country music's biggest stars and promising young musicians together for music and talk. The interviewing dynamo then began his own production company, which brought viewers TNN's highly successful *On the Record*. Currently Emery produces *The Nashville Show*, a weekly Webcast that he co-hosts with his old *Nashville Now* puppet sidekick, Shotgun Red. Known for his warm and gracious demeanor both on- and offscreen, the Disc Jockey Hall of Famer has written several best-selling books about his experiences discovering some of country music's biggest stars.

My year-round job was to bring in the chopped wood for the stove. I was a big believer in Santa Claus, and you can bet that when December came around, I was hauling that wood as fast as I could. Every Christmas Eve, our family came over for dinner and presents. Our tree was beautiful, even without electric lights. It had angel hair strewn from top to bottom and ornaments sparkling from every branch. It was the most gorgeous thing I'd ever seen. At the end of the evening you'd hear a loud knock at the door. "Who's that? What's that?" People looked at the door, then at me: "Ralph, go to the door." I'd open the door, and there would be Santa Claus! Bigger than life, standing right in front of me. I was a bit scared of him; after all, this was the guy who'd been watching me haul the wood all year long, and I didn't know if I'd be on his naughty or nice list, but he was always very kind. One Christmas, when I was about eight years old, I peeked into the kitchen at the wrong time. There was my grandfather putting the Santa suit on. Nobody saw me, and that night when they sent me to the door, I knew it has him. But I didn't want to ruin everyone's Christmas, so I played along. Later that night, I talked to my grandmother. She told me my grandfather had been Santa all along, but that they did it because they loved me. And I certainly felt loved in my grandparents' home.

My parents had divorced when I was four, so I was raised down on the farm by my grandparents for several years. My grandfather, the postmaster of McEwen, Tennessee, really became my father. Thursday was our day. He would take the afternoon off to go fishing and swimming with me in Hurricane Creek. He also taught me how to shoot a .22 rifle—I wasn't a bad shot—and we went rabbit hunting together.

Radio was king back then. On a battery-powered radio, we listened to the *Grand Ole Opry*, as most people in the South did. Of course, WSM—as I came to know later when I worked there—had a reach across the entire eastern United States. The three major broadcasting events of that era were the fireside talks of President Roosevelt, the Joe Louis fight, and the *Grand Ole Opry*. We listened to all of them.

We went to the Church of Christ, where my grandmother and grandfather were the church leaders. With a congregation of fifteen members, we couldn't afford a preacher. Except for one special day in the summer when we'd have a sermon by a real preacher, followed by an enormous feast. Country cooks would come from miles around bringing fried chicken and homemade pies and cakes. Country ham was always my favorite. Oh, and green beans, too. I've always been a vegetable man, but the beans had to be cooked country-style—in lots and lots of grease.

Living in McEwen was like living on another planet. We had a smokehouse instead of refrigeration and used kerosene lamps—with special white gas lamps on Sunday—instead of electricity. A well pumped the water out of the ground, and we had one running spigot. When August came, all the neighborhood ladies brought the vegetables in from the field and canned them all day long. Apples, peaches, beans—during the Depression if you could grow your own food, you wouldn't starve. When I wasn't doing chores, I was outside playing cowboys and Indians—if you were lucky, you had a cap pistol, otherwise you'd just get a corked stick and run around yelling, "Pow! Pow!" Down by the creek, I placed empty tin cans between rocks and waited for crawfish to make their nests in there. After a week, those tin cans were just full of big crawfish.

One of my most vivid memories happened on August 15, 1945—VJ Day. All the kids in McEwen got together and found the biggest American flag you've ever seen. We put it on a pole and paraded it all over town. Everyone came out and started celebrating the end of the war and our guys coming home. The war had so much of an impact in that little town. The war was a total effort, and everyone had someone fighting over there. Everything was rationed, and everyone was making some kind of sacrifice. When the war was over, people were thrilled, running around town, hugging each other, and celebrating in the streets. It was an amazing time, and I couldn't have asked for a better childhood than living with my grandparents in that little country town.

Sara Evans

The oldest girl among seven children, Sara Evans was raised on a farm near New Franklin, Missouri, and music was a major part of her life from the time she could walk. At five years old, she was already singing in her family's band and performing at American Legion halls, talent contests, and PTA meetings. By the time she was sixteen, she was performing in nightclubs. In 1991, Sara packed up and moved to Nashville to become a country music artist. Fate came knocking when Harlan Howard, country music's preeminent composer, heard her singing his classic "I've Got a Tiger by the Tail" on a demo tape. Claiming he'd found the voice he'd been looking for, the legendary songwriter led Sara to RCA. Her debut album, *Three Chords and the Truth*, won critical acclaim but didn't burst onto mainstream country radio. Her second album, *No Place That Far*, exploded into heavy rotation with its hit title track, but it was her third album, *Born to Fly*, that truly shot Sara to the top. Released in 2000, the album went on to be a double-platinum hit, earning her a Country Music Association Album of the Year nomination and a CMA award for Video of the Year. In 2003, Sara released *Restless*, an album that went platinum and led to her being the most played female singer on country music radio. With the release of her fifth album in 2005, *Real Fine Place*, Sara again soared to the top of both country and pop charts, resulting in two CMA award nominations, including Female Vocalist of the Year. Despite her stardom, Sara, whose definition of entourage is bringing her three young children on the road, remains a country girl at heart.

I grew up country. And I mean *country*. It was rural living on a tobacco farm with seven kids and a mother who was so old-fashioned she was almost Amish. I grew up in the 1980s, but it felt like the 1960s. We spent our days working on the farm, separating cattle on horseback, feeding the pigs and cattle, hauling hay, hanging clothes on the line, setting tobacco in the field—the work was constant. No wonder my mom had so many kids. In kindergarten, all the country kids went to school in the morning, and the town kids went in the afternoon, a long-standing tradition that freed the country kids to help on the farm in the afternoons. I'd come into the house at night after my chores were done, eat supper with my family around nine o'clock, and fall into bed at night completely exhausted. It was truly hard work, but it was a spectacular way to grow up.

The simple things were the best, like the once-a-week trip to the grocery store, our regular Friday night trips to Dairy Queen, Saturday nights gathered around the radio listening to the *Grand Ole Opry*, and of course my mom's amazing breakfasts on Christmas mornings. Up at five o'clock, before the sun came out, she was in the kitchen making the most delicious feast from scratch—cinnamon rolls, sausage, eggs, bacon, toast, biscuits, and gravy. We'd wake up early, gorge that food, and open our gifts while still wearing the new pj's our granny had given us the night before. Then the guys would go hunting while the kids played outside. After a full day, we'd return home to yet another homemade feast of ham, macaroni and cheese, and mashed potatoes. My mom has pulled off this feat every single year with a tiny kitchen and no dishwasher. Even when I was little, I knew what an amazing homemaker she was, and I tried to learn by her side whenever I could. Not surprisingly, my favorite Christmas present was an Easy-

Bake Oven waiting for me under the sparkling tree when I was five years old.

People who grow up on a farm are so blessed. They experience things city kids don't. They know what a good day of hard work feels like, they have a connection to nature and animals, they have a deeply ingrained work ethic, and they understand the importance of appreciating the small things in life. I have my own family now, and we don't live on a farm, but I'm doing my very best to bring a taste of country living to the suburbs, to teach my kids those vitally important life lessons and values I was so fortunate to learn on the family farm.

Dobie Gray

Dobie Gray was born to a family of sharecroppers outside of Houston, Texas, and his early life revolved around family, church, and music. His lifelong interest in gospel music was fostered by his grandfather, a Baptist minister. A versatile vocalist and songwriter who could handle soul, country, and pop with impressive ease, Dobie moved to Los Angeles in the 1960s to seek his fortune. He found it. His first chart-hit success came in 1963 with "Look at Me," followed two years later by the release of the wildly successful "The In Crowd." His biggest recording success came with 1973's "Drift Away," a song that broke into the Top 5 and remains a radio favorite today. With his move to Nashville, Dobie melded his country and gospel roots, and his fruitful songwriting career took off, composing songs for Ray Charles, Johnny Mathis, George Jones, Nina Simone, Conway Twitty, John Conlee, and Tammy Wynette, among many others. But the man who is known as a "songwriter's songwriter" still finds the time to head to the recording studio. His latest projects include a reworking of vintage R & B and 1960s hits on *Soul Days* and a collection of Christmas favorites on *Songs of the Season*. The prodigious talent sums it up best: "My goal is, and always will be, to make music that comes straight from the heart."

In Simonton, Texas, *town* was the cotton gin, the filling station, Luke Cini's Beer Joint, and two dry-goods stores: Daley's and

Simpson's, where the scent of sawdust, linseed oil, pecans, bologna, root beer, links of smoked sausage, and slabs of salt pork, hanging from the rafters, was always in the air. Heavy on practicalities, light on frills, Daley's and Simpson's stocked everything from potbellied stoves and plow shears to blackstrap molasses and girdles. A corner in Simpson's was also our post office. Arrival of the new Sears and Roebuck catalog was cause for celebration. Its ultrathin black-and-white pages filled with tempting new things to order had the power to transport. Color ads, printed on slick, bonded paper, were interspersed and featured beautiful models in togs and settings as inaccessible as the moon. By and by, the well-turned pages took their final licks in the *backhouza*— used sparingly. The glossies—well crumpled, owing to their sturdiness—were last to the split (a.k.a. your rear end). Then there was the long wait for that next issue—come on, April!

Ron Kingery

A former sound engineer whose work garnered a Grammy nomination, Ron Kingery joined musical forces with Scott Whitehead after they met at a Nashville songwriter showcase. Both grew up in military families where an indefatigable work ethic was of paramount importance. With unwavering determination, the two founded Hometown News. With their synchronized two-part harmony, Ron and Scott have earned comparisons to music legends like the Bellamy Brothers and Simon & Garfunkel. But this duo, who now add "producer" to their credit line, have a sound all their own. With their debut album, *Wheels*, Hometown News offers a slice of real life for their listeners to devour. Whether it's grind the workingman's in "Revitalize" or the poignancy of the circle of life in "Wheels," Hometown News never fail to deliver the real deal. Since their introduction to the country music audience with their debut Top 40 single, "Minivan," they have toured military bases around the world, made their Grand Ole Opry debut, and been nominated for the Academy of Country Music's Top Vocal Duo Award.

My childhood memories today seem like a series of snapshots. These snapshots are not merely photographs but more like video clips that encompass all of my senses. You know what I mean. Just close your eyes for a moment and imagine standing out by your grandma's clothesline on a breezy summer day. There's nothing like the smell of fresh clean clothes on the line mixed with the aroma of honeysuckle and fresh-cut clover hay. That's what I'm talking about.

Growing up in the country was something I took for granted as a child. I realize that now that I live smack-dab in the middle of Nashville. I miss the sound of frogs, insects, and whip-poor-wills, letting me know that the day has come to an end. I miss waving at total strangers and having them smile and wave back. All in all, I just miss the country.

Being a country boy, I learned how to entertain myself as a child. My brothers and I could always find something fun to do. We couldn't always make it into town to the swimming pool, so we simply swam in ponds and creeks. Once we made our own Slip 'n Slide out of plastic garbage bags. We even made a sail for our johnboat out of those same garbage bags. When we went fishing, we didn't have a bait store close by, so we used what was on hand. Grasshoppers, crickets, worms, grubs, even baby snakes were a part of our fishing arsenal. Of course we went frog gigging in the evenings. During the winter we would slip out to the fields and hunt quail and rabbits. Sometimes we just explored. No matter what season it was, we always found something to do, and it was always done outdoors. You would never find one of the Kingery brothers indoors watching TV or playing video games. No sir. My folks would have to whistle or honk the car horn just to round us all up in the evening. We truly loved living in the country.

Summertime in the country wasn't always fun and games for us. As children we worked. Many of us worked for farmers. We fed livestock, baled hay, sprayed weed killer, cut weeds out of bean fields, and worked in seed houses. Of course we mowed our own yards, split and stacked firewood, fed our dogs and horses, and did any other chore that Dad could think of. He knew that if we stayed busy, trouble wouldn't be as apt to find us.

Today, when I visit my hometown, I still like to drive down that old blacktop road where I used to live. I think back on the many trips I took down that road as a child. I think about the times I went down that road on a hay wagon or a tractor. I think about the time when my buddy pulled me down that road on my skateboard with his motorcycle. (I fell and got a concussion, so, kids, don't try that at home!) I think about how quiet that road was when I rode my bicycle into town. I think about little Tonya Gilpin, who was hit by a car and killed while riding her bicycle on that very road. Most of all I think back on the pleasant feelings I had when we'd turn in to our gravel driveway. The sound of that gravel on our tires was the best sound in the world. That sound meant that I was home. Home in the country.

Charging into his sixth decade of hit making with a magnificent track record that includes twenty BMI awards, six Million-Air awards, and a stellar reputation as one of the most consistently creative and soulful writers, Dickey Lee is truly a treasure in American music. Getting his start at the legendary Sun Records in Memphis, Tennessee, the same label that was putting out records by Elvis Presley, Jerry Lee Lewis, and Johnny Cash, Dickey made his own mark with classics like "Patches," "Laurie," and "I Saw Linda Yesterday." An immensely talented songwriter, Dickey has been responsible for writing some of country music's greatest hits, including "She Thinks I Still Care," which would soar to No. 1 and become yet another country classic to add to his long list of achievements. Today, the Nashville Songwriters Hall of Famer spends his time writing for such superstar artists as Reba McEntire, George Strait, Tracy Byrd, and Kathy Mattea. When asked what he will do when he retires, this powerhouse hit maker replied, "I guess I'll just keep on doing what I'm doing as a hobby. It's a blessing from God to get paid for what you love to do."

ey, Mom and Dad, Rocky Krsnich is coming over for Sunday dinner," I said casually.

"What?" They looked at me in disbelief. "Are you crazy?"

"No, it's true. He and his wife are coming over," I said, beaming at them.

Earlier that day, I'd gone to a Memphis Chicks baseball game. As the AA affiliate of the Chicago White Sox, the Chicks were local celebrities and their games were one of the most exciting sports events around. After the game, I had waited outside the locker room for the players to come out. Rocky Krsnich, who wore number six and was my favorite ballplayer, emerged from the locker room, and before I knew it, I had walked right up to him. "Mr. Krsnich," I said, "you're my favorite baseball player. Is there any chance you could come to my house and have dinner?" At the time, guys in the minor leagues weren't making much money, so the invitation for a home-cooked meal wasn't easy to turn down. Sure enough, Sunday came and a cab rolled up in front of our house. Rocky and his wife, Marie, came for dinner! My dad had built a baseball diamond on our farm with a tractor, and I spent countless days playing ball with my friends on that field. And now I had a professional ballplayer at my house throwing the ball around with me on the baseball diamond. It didn't get much better than that. In fact, it was so unreal I even got into a fight at school the following day because a kid didn't believe me. Rocky was later traded to the Cincinnati Reds and I lost track of him, but I'll never forget the best Sunday dinner of my childhood.

Dwayne O'Brien

An award-winning, Grammy-nominated singer-songwriter, Dwayne O'Brien was raised in rural Oklahoma, where he grew up with a love for music and aviation, both passed down from his father, a pilot. After college, Dwayne, who earned a bachelor's degree in chemistry and a master's degree in the communication of science, engineering, and technology from Vanderbilt University, moved to Nashville to try his hand at music and formed the band Little Texas. Known as the "hardest working band in country music," they often played over three hundred shows a year without a bus, without a driver, and without tour support from a label. Their never-say-die attitude paid off. With three No. 1 hits, "What Might Have Been," "God Blessed Texas," and "My Love," as well as a long list of Top 5s and Top 10s throughout the 1990s, the group was rocketed to superstardom and multiplatinum status. Garnering praise from fans and critics alike, the band has been showered with the industry's top accolades, including the Academy of Country Music's award for Vocal Group of the Year, Country Music Television's award for Video of the Year, and the Country Music Association's award for Album of the Year for their contribution to *Common Thread: The Songs of the Eagles*. After taking some well-deserved time off, Little Texas is back and continuing to pack stadiums at every tour stop. As a songwriter, Dwayne has won a number of prestigious ASCAP awards, including Crossover Song of the Year for "What Might Have Been." His astounding singing and songwriting success has enabled Dwayne to pursue his passion for aviation, and the two loves that were passed down from his father have been flawlessly combined in his self-penned solo album, *Song Pilot*.

I am and will forever be thankful that I was born and raised in the small country town of Ada, Oklahoma. Tucked away in the southeast part of the state, Ada sits among the post oaks and blackjacks where the red clay riverbeds carve wandering oxbows across the rolling green skin of the land. It's a town with one middle school, one high school, one post office, and many churches. It's a place where common sense is still pretty common. Now that I have lived away from there for some time and have seen a good part of the world, it has become more apparent just how greatly my view of the world has been shaped by that little town, and just how much I have to be thankful for.

I'm thankful to have been born to a hardworking father and a praying mother. There were many times that work was scarce and times were hard, but Momma always found a way to have good food on the table. I'm thankful that although my parents could not pay my way in this world, they gave me all that I needed in order to find my way on my own. They didn't have much, but I have the tremendous blessing of knowing that they gave me all they had.

I'm thankful that our house was on the edge of town and right next to a creek that was a young boy's delight. On its honeysuckle-covered banks, I would fish for perch by day and run laughing through swarms of fireflies in the long summer twilight. I'm also thankful that I grew up before video games.

I'm thankful for Main Street and the parades where I learned very young to salute the flag as it was carried past by veterans who'd gone off from my little town to fight in faraway places with names like the Argonne, Anzio, Normandy, and Hue. To this day,

I'm grateful to all who wear the uniform of the U.S. military. God bless them all, and all who wait for their safe return.

I'm thankful that Main Street still has places like Folger's Drive-In—undoubtedly the best hamburger joint in the world and to a great degree the very heart of the town. On its dozen or so cracked turquoise bar stools sit farmers, teachers, bank presidents, and oil-field roughnecks—all catching up on the latest and all on a first-name basis. Invariably, the conversation turns to how the senior class looks and how the football team will do at state this year. It's the kind of place where you don't even have to order. As soon as you order a few times, your face is your order. To this day, it's the first place I go when I hit town, and moments after I sit down, a cheeseburger basket—no onions and an unsweetened iced tea—will appear as if by magic. Maybe it is.

I'm thankful for the good education I received at my public schools, and thankful that my kindergarten graduation photo has the same faces as my high school graduation photo. I'm also thankful that when I wore my school's uniform, it bore the name of my town as well.

I'm thankful for places like Kiwanis Field—the only baseball field in town and where all of the Little League games were watched by parents who were themselves teammates on the very same patch of dirt. And for characters like Sonny—a gentle giant of a man slow of speech and mind but quick to love and encourage. He had watched my older brothers' generation play baseball and was there to watch mine. He knew my name, the teams I had played for, that I threw right-handed and batted left, and that I usually pulled the ball from swinging too hard. He would stand behind the chain link of the backstop cheering on every batter on every single team. And after the game, he was right there offering a labored "Good game" to every player. Never married and childless, but no matter; Sonny had the whole town for a family.

I'm thankful every time I get to go back there to visit, but I'm even more thankful that Ada goes with me wherever I go in this world. I'm a product of its genuine people, its simple lifestyle, and its resilient character, and I've never been more proud of anything in my life than to call it home.

That little town has become even more sacred ground now that my mother, father, and a dear sister rest in peace on a hillside just outside of town. But I know not just where they are but where they wait, and that I will see them again.

Ada is the kind of place where kids grow up, move away, and then, more times than not, come back to raise their own families. I'm one of the few who have not. But then again, I go back quite often. For it's never long before my mind takes a familiar and well-worn path to a time and place where all is right and good: where I still swing for the bleachers at Kiwanis Field, and Sonny still cheers; the honeysuckle hangs heavy in the soft summer twilight, and Momma always has dinner waiting.

Dolly Parton

Born the fourth of twelve children, international superstar Dolly Parton grew up in a run-down one-room cabin in the Great Smoky Mountains. With a grandfather who was a Pentecostal preacher and parents who were devout parishioners in the Assembly of God church, Dolly had a childhood that revolved around spiritual music. As a child, she began singing on local radio shows, and by the time she was thirteen, she wasn't just listening to the *Grand Ole Opry*—she was appearing on the Opry's stage. After high school, she brought her irrepressible rural east Tennessee spirit of folklore and fun to Nashville. She soon found success as a prolific songwriter and broke out as a solo vocalist in 1974. She holds twenty-five U.S. gold, platinum, and multiplatinum honors and has seen twenty-five songs reach No. 1 on the *Billboard* charts. The recipient of seven Grammy awards, she is one of only five solo women to win the Country Music Association's highest honor of Entertainer of the Year.

guess most people can't imagine being anything other than what they are. And in my case, that's country. I can't imagine what my life would have been without peaceful days, mountain streams, homegrown and home-cooked food, country church, and all-day singing with dinner on the grounds with family and friends. It is all that keeps me sane in an otherwise crazy world these days.

ABOUT THE EDITOR

Legendary country superstar and fiddle-playing virtuoso Charlie Daniels has been a music icon for over forty years and has become an integral part of the American popular culture. CDB music, as Charlie likes to call it, is an exhilarating mixture of rock, country, bluegrass, blues, and gospel. Although geared to the mind-set of the Southern lifestyle, Charlie strikes a chord with all Americans since his music can be rebel rousing with the spirit that embraces the American ideal. Charlie's energy and strong support for our nation is evidenced by his many accolades. His volunteer spirit and down-to-earth philosophy exemplify this true American patriot.